RTI

RTI

A Practitioner's Guide to Implementing
Response to Intervention

Daryl F. Mellard
Evelyn Johnson

A JOINT PUBLICATION

CORWIN PRESS
A SAGE Publications Company
Thousand Oaks, CA 91320

NATIONAL ASSOCIATION OF ELEMENTARY SCHOOL PRINCIPALS
Serving All Elementary and Middle Level Principals

For information:

Corwin Press
A Sage Publications Company
2455 Teller Road
Thousand Oaks, California 91320
www.corwinpress.com

Sage Publications India Pvt. Ltd.
B 1/I 1 Mohan Cooperative
   Industrial Area
Mathura Road, New Delhi 110 044
India

Sage Publications Ltd.
1 Oliver's Yard
55 City Road
London EC1Y 1SP
United Kingdom

Sage Publications Asia-Pacific Pte. Ltd.
33 Pekin Street #02–01
Far East Square
Singapore 048763

Printed in the United States of America

Library of Congress Cataloging-in-Publication Data

Mellard, Daryl F. (Daryl Francis), 1950–
RTI: A practitioner's guide to implementing response to intervention/Daryl F. Mellard, Evelyn Johnson.
    p. cm.
Includes bibliographical references and index.
ISBN-13: 978-1-4129-5771-7 (cloth)
ISBN-13: 978-1-4129-5772-4 (pbk.)
    1. Remedial teaching. 2. Slow learning children—Education. 3. Learning disabled children—Education. I. Johnson, Evelyn. II. Title. III. Title: Response to intervention. IV. Title: Practitioner's guide to implementing response to intervention.

LB1029.R4M45 2008
371.9—dc22   2007015255

This book is printed on acid-free paper.

07   08   09   10   11   10   9   8   7   6   5   4   3   2   1

Acquisitions Editor:	Allyson P. Sharp
Editorial Assistant:	Mary Dang
Production Editor:	Melanie Birdsall
Copy Editor:	Alison Hope
Typesetter:	C&M Digitals (P) Ltd.
Proofreader:	Dennis W. Webb
Indexer:	Ellen Slavitz
Cover Designer:	Monique Hahn
Graphic Designer:	Lisa Miller

Contents

Preface

Response to intervention (RTI) is gaining momentum as a school-wide framework for improving students' outcomes; an increasing number of resources describe RTI. The purpose of this text is to provide practical guidance on implementing an RTI framework within a school. Developing and implementing RTI is not a one-shot, quick-fix activity. It involves important social, technical, and practical considerations. As state education agencies, school districts, and school staffs develop and implement RTI, this text will provide a framework for understanding the components, procedures, practices, and criteria that are reflected in research. We believe that the most significant issues that implementers confront are not technical but social. Successful implementation requires ensuring a fit with the personal views, interaction patterns, and contextual features of a school's climate. The text's guidance will help with those decisions that support RTI within the varied contexts of states' and schools' policies and practices.

Clarifying our perspective in writing this text is important. As described in Chapter 1, RTI can serve three distinct applications: screening and prevention, early intervention, and disability determination. Within this text, we emphasize RTI in a general education setting for prevention and early intervention of students' learning difficulties. Strong evidence supports the RTI components and principles to improve instruction and related student outcomes. The research does not, to date, support the use of RTI as an exclusive component to disability determination. However, the research foundation may be used in incorporating RTI as *one* component of disability determination. As such, RTI provides documentation that the student has received appropriate and high-quality instruction in the general classroom, but more thorough assessment is required to determine the nature and extent of the student's disability if a special education referral is made.

The suggestions and guidance presented are drawn extensively from the National Research Center on Learning Disabilities (NRCLD) research. Like many areas of education, research and understanding of areas related to RTI continue to expand at incredible rates. In recognition of this expanding knowledge, rather than recommending specific curricula or assessment tools, or both, that may quickly become outdated or limited in scope, we have attempted to capture the salient features, characteristics, and principles on which research-based RTI models are based. Understanding these principles may help a school make decisions as new curricula, screening measures, progress monitoring systems, and intervention tools are developed. We intend for schools to find the information useful as they begin their RTI model development and implementation.

The information is organized into nine chapters. Chapters 1 and 2 provide an overview of the RTI framework, as well as the policies and legislation that support its implementation. Chapters 3 through 8 are devoted to explaining the particular components of a three-tiered RTI model: Schoolwide Screening, Progress Monitoring, Tier 1: General Education, Tier 2: Intervention, Tier 3: Special Education, and Fidelity of Implementation. Within each of these chapters, you will find definitions, features, implementation guidance, case studies, and resources to facilitate your understanding and planning. Finally, Chapter 9 summarizes what is currently known about RTI and offers concluding thoughts on implementation.

Acknowledgments

This work would not have been possible without significant contributions from many professionals in the field, including our colleagues at the NRCLD: Don Deshler, Doug Fuchs, Lynn Fuchs, Don Compton, Dan Reschly, Barbara Starrett, Melinda McKnight, Julie Tollefson, Sonja de Boer, and Sara Byrd; Lou Danielson and Renee Bradley from the Office of Special Education Programs (OSEP); the school staffs from Jefferson Elementary School in Pella, Iowa, Tualatin Elementary in Tualatin, Oregon, Rosewood Elementary School in Vero Beach, Florida, and Northstar Elementary School in Knoxville, Iowa. Finally, we acknowledge the editorial work of Kirsten McBride, whose talents in translating jargon, obfuscations, and other confusions into meaningfully connected prose are incredible and are greatly appreciated.

The grant from Office of Special Education Programs (OSEP) in the U.S. Department of Education (Award #324U010004) that funded the NRCLD helped support the research underlying this book. The contents are solely the responsibility of the authors and do not necessarily represent the official views of OSEP.

Publisher's Acknowledgments

Corwin Press gratefully acknowledges the following reviewers for their contributions to this book:

John La Londe
Director
Marin Special Education Local Plan Area
San Rafael, CA

Roger Piwowarski
School Psychologist
Harrison School District Two
Department of Special Programs
Colorado Springs, CO

Sancta Sorensen
Special Education and Pre-Algebra Teacher
Monroe Middle School
Omaha, NE

Karen L. Tichy
Associate Superintendent for Instruction
Catholic Education Office
St. Louis, MO

About the Authors

 **Daryl F. Mellard,** PhD (University of Kansas), began his career in school psychology. Since 1982, Dr. Mellard has been a research associate within the Center for Research on Learning and the Division of Adult Studies. He is the director of the Division of Adult Studies, which includes a professional staff of 12 and approximately 35 student research assistants. The Division's work examines policies and practices that limit the abilities of adults with disabilities to fully participate in society's everyday activities.

He has been the principal investigator of research and evaluation studies. Dr. Mellard's current projects address assessment and services to children and youth with learning disabilities, reading comprehension, and adult literacy. Dr. Mellard is one of the principal investigators with the National Research Center on Learning Disabilities (NRCLD) (nrcld.org) that examined the identification of learning disabilities, including the application of responsiveness to intervention. Dr. Mellard directed the NRCLD staff in their review of RTI as implemented in numerous elementary school settings. Dr. Mellard also directed research on social, education, and employment issues for adults with disabilities. These projects involved consumers, employers, and staff in community and technical colleges, independent living centers, vocational rehabilitation, One-Stop Career Centers, and adult education and literacy programs.

Additionally, as a service to the state of Kansas, Dr. Mellard served as a co-chair to the Kansas Coalition on Adult Literacy and Learning Disabilities. This work group was formed to coordinate the efforts of education, corrections, rehabilitation, human resources, and businesses in meeting the needs and legal requirements of individuals with disabilities. Contributing to his views on adults with disabilities and their services, for the past six years Dr. Mellard has served as an officer on a board of directors' for the local independent living center.

 **Evelyn Johnson,** EdD (Boise State University), was a research associate for the National Research Center on Learning Disabilities (NRCLD) (nrcld.org) until August 2007, at which time she began work as an Assistant Professor of Special Education at Boise State University in Boise, Idaho. She began her career in Washington in 1994 as a special education teacher, and then at the University of Washington, Seattle, where her research focused on the inclusion of students with disabilities in accountability systems. Dr. Johnson's work on assessment for students with disabilities has included research on accommodations and alternative assessments, as well as investigations on literacy assessment. She worked for the NRCLD from 2003 to 2007, during which time she developed numerous technical assistance products to assist state and local educational agencies on RTI and learning disability identification–related issues.

1

Introduction

What Is RTI?

Response to intervention (RTI) is a promising new process of instruction, assessment, and intervention that allows schools to identify struggling students early, provide appropriate instructional interventions, and increase the likelihood that the students can be successful and maintain their class placement. RTI, when implemented according to best practices, addresses many shortcomings of current systems of identifying students that are at risk for learning disabilities (LDs) and providing appropriate interventions. Traditionally, schools have had two parallel systems for students: general and special education. A student who was perceived to be unsuccessful in the general classroom was referred for evaluation for special education services, and, if found eligible, was frequently served under the category of learning disabled. Special education was typically a separate system of instruction, with little alignment to the general curriculum. Additionally, evaluation procedures for students with LDs resulted in a "wait to fail" model, because of the need to demonstrate a discrepancy between aptitude and achievement. RTI addresses many of these shortcomings. Through its focus on alignment of general classroom instruction, progress monitoring, and evidence-based interventions, RTI can help schools work more efficiently and effectively in addressing the needs of all learners.

RTI provides a process through which the achievement of all students can be enhanced. The RTI framework is also consistent with current federal and state policies that focus on improving outcomes for all students and on increasing access to the general curriculum. For example, RTI can be used to meet the requirements outlined in the Individuals with Disabilities Education Act (IDEA, 2004) for determination of specific learning disabilities (SLDs). The closer alignment of interventions with general classroom instruction in the RTI process also provides a mechanism through which schools ensure access to the general curriculum for all students. Additionally, the focus in RTI on progress monitoring, early intervention, and evidence-based practices is consistent with many of the requirements of the No Child Left Behind Act (NCLB, 2001) and Reading First policies. Most important, when implemented with fidelity, RTI procedures can identify and intervene for struggling students early in the educational process, thereby reducing academic failure. For example, numerous screening measures for reading failure can be used with kindergarteners and first graders and can accurately identify those students who are most at risk for reading failure. For these students, instructional and curricular changes can be made to increase their likelihood of success (Catts, 2006; Compton, 2006).

Our goal in this text is to provide a guide to school-level implementation of RTI that is based on a review of school- and research-based RTI practices and procedures (see, for example, Bradley, Danielson, & Hallahan, 2002; NRCLD, 2003; Vaughn & Fuchs, 2003). It is our hope that the text is a useful tool for school-level leaders as they begin the process of implementation. To accomplish this, we've organized this text in three main sections: (a) an overview to describe the concept of RTI and its relation to existing policy initiatives (Chapters 1 and 2); (b) a detailed guide to implementation based on research-based components of an RTI model, including descriptions of actual implementation sites (Chapters 3 through 8); and (c) a summary of the research and continuing questions on RTI (Chapter 9). Finally, the text includes numerous resources for pursuing further information. Overall, we believe you will find this text helpful as you consider RTI implementation. The practical descriptions and multiple examples will increase the ease with which you will be able to thoughtfully, accurately, and effectively implement RTI within your school.

The remainder of this chapter includes a general description of how services are organized into tiers of increasing intensity within RTI, commonly recognized RTI components, the purposes of RTI, and research support for RTI.

RTI as a Three-Tiered Model

RTI is most often conceptualized as a multitiered model. This framework is based on a public health model of intervention whereby multiple tiers of increasingly intense interventions are directed at correspondingly smaller and smaller population segments. For example, in public health, the general population gets wellness information on how to stay healthy and receives basic, broad vaccinations. This represents the first, or primary, tier of intervention. Despite the efforts during the first tier, 10%–15% of the population may require treatment that is more specialized to stay healthy. This level of specialized treatment is considered the secondary level of intervention. Even within this second-tier group, about 5% will need very specialized interventions. This highest level is referred to as the tertiary level of intervention and is the most resource-intensive level.

When applied to students' academic performances, the three tiers are distinguished by their intervention focus. In Tier 1, all students receive high-quality, developmentally appropriate instruction within the general education classroom. Within this level, the environment is the most important component. Changes made in the instructional environment are considered to be most valuable for improving the overall student performance; since these changes can be anticipated on the basis of previous experience and research findings, much effort is directed at improving the general education environment. General education staff conduct screenings to identify students at risk for academic failure and to ensure that all students are benefiting from instruction. Students whose screening results indicate that they are not making adequate progress receive appropriate interventions in Tier 2. Tier 2 interventions typically involve small-group instruction on the targeted area of deficit. For example, students who have difficulty decoding words will receive intense, small-group instruction that is focused on this skill. The frequency (number of minutes a day, number of days a week) and duration (how many weeks) of the intervention are usually specified as conditions for the Tier 2 intervention. The student's response to this intervention is monitored; based on this response, one of three decisions is made: (1) If the student is at a level of performance that matches that of his grade-level peers, he returns to Tier 1. (2) If the student's performance is still below that of his grade-level peers, but he is making adequate progress toward the stated goals, the student may remain in a Tier 2 intervention. Finally, (3) if the student does not respond to the intervention provided, he moves to Tier 3, where interventions that are more intensive can be provided to meet individual needs.

Two features distinguish Tier 3 interventions: First, they are no longer considered interventions to prevent, but rather as interventions to address an identified need. Second, they are generally individual focused, and not group focused as in Tiers 1 and 2. Interventions at Tier 3 are considered the most powerful available, which is often reflected in the severity of the disability of the individuals receiving the intervention, the quality of the instructor, and the interventions' demonstrated effectiveness. The instructional intensity, curriculum, instructional goals, and instructional setting may all be manipulated to increase the likelihood of the student responding successfully. Figure 1.1 depicts a three-tiered RTI model.

RTI reflects an integration of several concepts important to improving learners' outcomes and to improving the accuracy of the diagnosis of LDs. RTI combines important features of assessment and instruction to address the limitations associated with current intervention and assessment models. Among the commonly cited limitations with current approaches to LD determination is that assessments may not accurately reflect the curricular tasks students confront in their classroom and that they provide a very narrow view of students' knowledge, skills, and abilities. In contrast, RTI has highly contextualized assessment such as judging student performance in light of the curricular demands within a school or district and focusing assessment tasks on those tasks that very closely match those that a student is confronting in the classroom. These features help increase the ecological validity of the assessment. The following are core requirements of a strong RTI model:

1. *High-Quality, Research-Based Classroom Instruction.* All students receive high-quality instruction in the general education setting. General education instruction is research based; general

Figure 1.1   Three-Tiered RTI Model

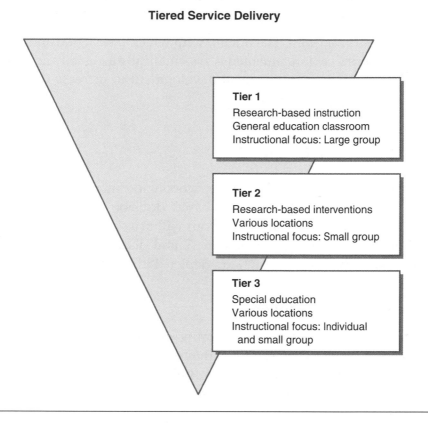

Tiered Service Delivery

Tier 1
Research-based instruction
General education classroom
Instructional focus: Large group

Tier 2
Research-based interventions
Various locations
Instructional focus: Small group

Tier 3
Special education
Various locations
Instructional focus: Individual
   and small group

education teachers assume an active role in students' assessment in the classroom curriculum.

2. *Universal Screening.* School staff, including the classroom teachers, conduct universal screening of academics and behavior. Specific criteria for judging the achievement of all students are applied in determining which students need closer monitoring or intervention.

3. *Progress Monitoring at All Tiers.* Progress monitoring is essential. In Tier 1, progress monitoring allows teachers to readily identify those learners who are not meeting expected standards. In Tiers 2 and 3, progress monitoring enables teachers to determine the interventions' effectiveness and to make changes as needed.

4. *Research-Based Interventions at Tiers 2 and 3.* When a student's screening or progress monitoring results indicate a deficit, an

appropriate instructional intervention is implemented. School staff implement specific, research-based interventions to address the student's difficulties.

5. *Fidelity Measures.* The fidelity with which instruction and interventions are implemented is systematically assessed and linked to continuing professional development to increase the effectiveness of the RTI process.

Purposes of RTI

Together, these components offer a schoolwide model of integrated instruction, assessment, and data-based decision making. The RTI model can serve three distinct functions within a school setting: screening and prevention, early intervention, and disability determination. The various applications of RTI are depicted in Figure 1.2.

Screening and Prevention

The focus on ensuring high-quality, evidenced-based instruction in the general education setting is the first line of defense in preventing later learning difficulties. When universal screening procedures identify students as being at risk, they may be targeted for further monitoring or for early intervention.

Figure 1.2   Applications of RTI

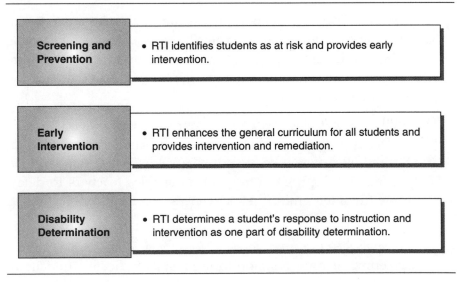

Early Intervention

Early intervention can occur at any grade level and is applied to students whose progress is not commensurate with that of their peers. The intent is to close the achievement and learning gaps and to intervene with an effective curricular and instructional change.

Disability Determination

RTI can serve as one important component of disability determination. The focus on evidenced-based instruction in general education, combined with research-based interventions in Tier 2, meets an important requirement of disability eligibility determination: that low achievement is not due to a lack of appropriate instructional experiences as described in IDEA 2004, 614 (b) (5). Thus, a student who fails to respond to research-based instruction and interventions should be further assessed to determine the presence of a disability. The data collected through progress monitoring on the student's performance, along with fidelity data to verify the instruction and interventions were appropriately implemented, serve as important evidence in the overall eligibility decision-making process.

Research Support for RTI

Research on an RTI framework has demonstrated the need and value for early identification of students with learning difficulties and for intense interventions delivered with fidelity. One of the most significant findings in the research on RTI is that the components and procedures used within this framework lend themselves to a better understanding of instructional quality and informed decision making (see, for example, Foorman, Francis, Fletcher, Schatschneider & Mehta, 1998; O'Connor & Jenkins, 1999; Torgesen, Alexander, Wagner, Rashotte, Voeller, & Conway, 2001). Instructional quality includes planning interventions, assessing intervention outcomes, and manipulating variables that are likely to improve outcomes. This feature has positive implications for teachers (both general and special education), parents, and staff. In addition, RTI can yield information that accurately ranks a student within his peer group and his performance in the school's curriculum (Speece & Case, 2001). As a result, students at risk for learning difficulties can be identified and receive appropriate interventions (Vaughn & Fuchs, 2003; Vaughn, Linan-Thompson, & Hickman, 2003).

For use within disability determination, some advocates of an RTI approach identify the following advantages of RTI:

- A reduced reliance on teachers to initiate referrals
- A focus on academic skills, not presumed processing deficits
- A focus on students' learning, not just current achievement
- The elimination of the need for aptitude-achievement discrepancy and intelligence testing
- A reduction in false positive identification errors (O'Connor, Harty, & Fulmer, 2005; Speece, Case & Molloy, 2003)

RTI is a multitiered framework for preventing reading problems and for intervening in the cases of students who are not successful in the general education curriculum. Numerous studies have demonstrated the effectiveness of RTI for preventing reading problems (summarized in Mellard, Byrd, Johnson, Tollefson, & Boesche, 2004). Controlled studies examining how RTI might be implemented by schools and districts within the process of disability determination demonstrate that RTI should be pursued as a viable option for identifying students with LDs (Speece et al., 2003; Vaughn et al., 2003). At this time, information from research-based interventions is primarily focused on early reading. Research examining the use of RTI in the areas of later reading, math, writing, and content areas is under way and will provide important information on how the RTI framework might be applied across content areas and grade levels.

Summary

RTI is an important construct because of its potential to help schools provide appropriate learning experiences for all students, and its use in the early identification of students at risk for academic failure. RTI is a multitiered service delivery intervention similar to those used for other schoolwide practices, such as positive behavioral support. RTI combines important features of assessment and instruction and consists of the following components:

1. High-quality, evidence-based instructional practices

2. Universal screening

3. Continuous progress monitoring of students in all tiers

4. Research-based interventions implemented with students identified as at risk

5. Fidelity of implementation

The research support for an RTI model demonstrates that it can lead to better instructional programming and decision making. Although current research focuses primarily on reading, RTI—as a framework—may be applied to other academic areas as the research base in these areas expands.

References

Bradley, R., Danielson, L., & Hallahan, D. P. (Eds.). (2002). *Identification of learning disabilities: Research to practice*. Mahwah, NJ: Lawrence Erlbaum.

Catts, H. W. (2006, April). Schoolwide screening. Presentation at the national SEA conference on responsiveness to intervention: Integrating RTI within the SLD determination process, Kansas City, MO. Retrieved July 12, 2006, from http://nrcld.org/sea/presentations_worksheets/screening/Catts_screening.pdf.

Compton, D. L. (2006, April 19). LD Identification within an RTI model: An overview of the tiered service delivery model. Retrieved November 2, 2006, from http://nrcld.org/sea/presentations_worksheets/tsd/Compton_TSD.pdf.

Foorman, B. R., Francis, D. J., Fletcher, J. M., Schatschneider, C., & Mehta, P. (1998). The role of instruction in learning to read: Preventing reading failure in at-risk children. *Journal of Educational Psychology, 90,* 37–55.

Individuals with Disabilities Education Act of 2004 (IDEA). (2004). Public Law 108-446.

Mellard, D. F., Byrd, S. E., Johnson, E., Tollefson, J. M., & Boesche, L. (2004). Foundations and research on identifying model responsiveness-to-intervention sites. *Learning Disability Quarterly, 27,* 243–256.

National Research Center on Learning Disabilities. (2003). NRCLD Symposium on RTI Retrieved October 15, 2006, from http://www.nrcld.org/symposium2003/index.html.

No Child Left Behind Act (NCLB). (2001). Public Law 107-110.

O'Connor, R. E., Harty, K. R., & Fulmer, D. (2005). Tiers of intervention in kindergarten through third grade. *Journal of Learning Disabilities, 38*(6), 532–538.

O'Connor, R., & Jenkins, J. R. (1999). The prediction of reading disabilities in kindergarten and first grade. *Scientific Studies of Reading, 3,* 159–197.

Speece, D. L., & Case, L. P. (2001). Classification in context: An alternative approach to identifying early reading disability. *Journal of Educational Psychology, 93*, 735–749.

Speece, D. L., Case, L. P., & Molloy, D. E. (2003). Responsiveness to general education instruction as the first gate to learning disabilities identification. *Learning Disabilities Research & Practice, 18*, 147–156.

Torgesen, J. K., Alexander, A. W., Wagner, R. K., Rashotte, C. A., Voeller, K. S., & Conway, T. (2001). Intensive remedial instruction for children with severe reading disabilities: Immediate and long-term outcomes from two instructional approaches. *Journal of Learning Disabilities, 34*, 33–58.

Vaughn, S., & Fuchs, L. S. (2003). Redefining learning disabilities as inadequate response to instruction: The promise and potential problems. *Learning Disabilities Research & Practice, 18*(3), 137–146.

Vaughn, S., Linan-Thompson, S., & Hickman, P. (2003). Response to instruction as a means of identifying students with reading/learning disabilities. *Exceptional Children, 69*(4), 391–409.

2

RTI in the Context of Policy Initiatives

R TI represents one of the many policy initiatives that compete for
a school's resources, attention, understanding, and implementation. For example, the No Child Left Behind Act (NCLB, 2001) and
Individuals with Disabilities Education Act (IDEA, 2004) include an
emphasis on accountability and the use of scientifically based curricula. In addition to these federal initiatives, state and local policies
related to assessment and instruction affect school functioning. Ultimately, most policy initiatives have a shared goal—improved learning for all students—although they often focus on a narrow aspect of
the curriculum, school functioning, or school population. Schools are
left to organize and integrate these policies in ways that complement
the school's stated mission to reach what has been called coherence
(Honig & Hatch, 2004; Newmann, Smith, Allensworth, & Bryk, 2001).
Coherence provides an organizing framework for schools to manage
the competing demands of policy initiatives while remaining faithful
to their stated mission.

Due to the numerous initiatives vying for attention, however,
policy incoherence is too often the norm for many schools as they
attempt to comply with competing demands. Incoherence occurs
when a particular policy is interpreted on its own, as if its practices

are unrelated to others (Spillane, Reiser & Reimer, 2002). The result is a fragmented, haphazard approach to ensuring a quality education for students.

In Chapter 1, we described the RTI framework, gave a description of its essential components, and discussed three uses for improving student outcomes. In this chapter, using policy coherence as a framework, we examine RTI within the context of three federal initiatives: NCLB 2001, Reading First, and IDEA 2004. We conclude the chapter with a table that juxtaposes these initiatives to highlight how they might be used efficiently and effectively to guide school improvement efforts.

Chapter at a Glance

Policy Coherence, Professional Learning Communities, and the Professional Teaching and Learning Cycle

At any given time, school leaders face the challenge of complying with numerous initiatives at the federal, state, and local levels. Examples include NCLB 2001, which places significant demands on instruction, assessment, and staffing requirements; IDEA 2004, which governs special education; changes to state curricula and assessment processes, which have resulted in significant changes to instruction; and changes in governance, such as school-based decision making. Although most policy initiatives are designed to address a significant problem such as increasing the number of highly qualified teachers, many are developed in isolation and narrowly defined, addressing a specific population, a specific academic or behavioral issue, or some other school function. However, addressing problems through solutions that are not coordinated with other efforts rarely results in the sustained improvements that schools hope to achieve (Herbert, Murphy, Ramos, Vaden-Kiernan, & Buttram, 2005). Many of these initiatives, especially at the federal level, offer inducements to schools whereby compliance with initiatives brings increased funding to support schools. Therefore, schools face a fundamental challenge of coordinating their efforts in a way that promotes increased student achievement and meets the demands of the policies that govern their school functioning.

Research on school improvement provides a helpful framework around which schools can organize their efforts in a way that leads to improved student achievement. This framework consists of three main components:

1. Deciding on the school's theory of purpose (described immediately below)

2. Creating coherence through the coordination of instructional efforts

3. Building the professional capacity of teachers and leaders (Herbert et al., 2005)

Theory of Purpose

Before any school improvement effort is undertaken, a school must decide what it stands for and what it hopes to achieve (Ashby, Maki, & Cunningham-Morris, 1996). Once articulated, this theory of purpose becomes the yardstick by which schools measure how well the policies they adopt contribute to and support their most important goals. Schools can then design appropriate courses of action that work toward supporting their goals. Many schools summarize their theory of purpose and frame it as a mission statement (Goodlad, Mantle-Bromley, & Goodlad, 2004). Thus, mission statements attempt to provide a concise vision of a school's purpose. A core feature of mission statements of successful school improvement sites is a focus on increased student learning and instructional improvement (Togneri & Anderson, 2003). To be meaningful, mission statements must guide all of the activities in which a school engages.

An RTI framework can be supportive of mission statements that focus on increased student learning and instructional improvement. RTI presents an integrated model of instruction, assessment, and intervention, as well as provides a schoolwide approach to reviewing and addressing academic achievement of all students.

Coherence

To be effective in increasing the goal of student achievement, a school must organize its functioning around this goal (Goodlad et al., 2004). Newmann et al. (2001) describe this organization as instructional program coherence (IPC), which is defined as "a set of interrelated programs for students and staff that are guided by a common framework for curriculum, instruction, assessment, and learning climate, and are pursued over a sustained period" (p. 299). According to Newmann and colleagues, schools that have high levels of IPC tend to have higher student achievement.

Key characteristics of IPC include the following:

1. Curriculum, instruction, assessment, and learning climates are coordinated, both within grade levels (horizontally) and across grade levels (vertically).

2. Support programs are coordinated with the school's instructional framework to support the needs of students at risk or struggling learners.

3. School organization is designed to support the implementation of this framework.

4. Materials, programs, and other resources are designed, allocated, and implemented in a manner consistent with the instructional framework (Newmann et al., 2001).

The RTI framework can help schools achieve greater instructional program coherence. Specifically, the alignment of screening instruments related to key academic areas in concert with the implementation of targeted interventions to support achievement in the general instructional program are useful instruments through which IPC can be achieved.

Building Capacity

How schools act to create and sustain higher levels of teacher performance is integral to implementing evidenced-based practices reliably to scale (Gerber, 2005). Professional learning communities (PLCs; Astuto, Clark, Read, McGree, & Fernandez, 1993; DuFour & Eaker, 1998) provide a model that has been demonstrated as effective for building instructional capacity that improves student achievement (Hord, 1997). Within a PLC, teachers and leaders build their capacity to

- Create IPC
- Use data systematically to inform and improve instruction
- Engage in continued professional development
- Build collaborative relationships that promote and support student achievement (DuFour & Eaker, 1998)

At the classroom level, an effective model for building capacity is the professional teaching and learning cycle (PTLC) (Herbert et al., 2005). Within the PTLC, teachers do the following:

1. Study the standards and set expectations for student learning

2. Select instructional practices to meet the expectations

3. Plan instruction and related, common assessments

4. Implement instruction and assessment

5. Analyze student performance

6. Adjust instruction according to results

Both the PLC and PTLC models provide helpful contexts for considering an RTI model. At the school level, RTI under the umbrella of PLC holds the promise of marked improvements in student achievement, the rapid identification of unproductive teaching techniques, and the prospect of informing professional development needs. At the classroom level, RTI and the PTLC emphasize the critical importance of monitoring, data-based decision making, and reflective practice.

Key Elements of NCLB 2001

The No Child Left Behind Act (NCLB, 2001) is one of the most significant federal education policy initiatives facing schools today. NCLB 2001 legislated significant changes in standards for schools that focus on accountability for every student's progress, ensuring that students are taught by highly qualified teachers, proving that programs are successful based on scientifically based research, and creating a system fully aligned with state learning regulations. Our goal here is not to provide a comprehensive review or critical analysis of NCLB, but rather to discuss specific components of the legislation that are relevant to RTI. Components of NCLB that are addressed through an RTI framework include

- Prevention of and intervention for academic problems
- Scientifically based research
- Accountability

Prevention and Intervention

NCLB 2001 is the reauthorization of the Elementary and Secondary Education Act (ESEA, 1965). ESEA was part of President Johnson's larger "war on poverty," which sought to improve educational opportunity for economically disadvantaged students. As part of the ESEA, Title I (Improving the Academic Achievement of the Disadvantaged) established a compensatory system of education devoted to improving the academic achievement of economically disadvantaged students. The purpose of Title I in NCLB was

> providing children an enriched and accelerated educational program, including the use of schoolwide programs or additional services that increase the amount and quality of instructional time; promoting schoolwide reform and ensuring the access of children to effective, scientifically based instructional strategies and challenging academic content. (NCLB, 2001, Sec. 1001(8), (9), p. 16)

One key purpose of an RTI process is a focus on intervention for students at risk for academic failure. That is, through screening and routine progress monitoring, students experiencing academic difficulties may be identified early and provided with specific interventions that increase their learning.

Scientifically Based Practice

Reviews of NCLB 2001 legislation often report the numerous references to scientifically based research and evidence-based practices. *Scientifically based research*, as defined in NCLB, "means research that involves the application of rigorous, systematic, and objective procedures to obtain reliable and valid knowledge relevant to education activities and programs" (NCLB, 2001, (37)(A), p. 540).

Two key components of effective RTI models include the use of evidence-based practices at all tiers of intervention and the use of progress monitoring, which has been demonstrated to result in improved academic outcomes (Stecker, Fuchs & Fuchs, 2005). Using an RTI framework across educational disciplines as well as grade levels is consistent with the focus on scientifically based research: it promotes the values that schools have an obligation to ensure that all students participate in strong instructional programs that support student achievement.

Accountability

Accountability is another large component of NCLB 2001, with its requirements that state education agencies submit reports detailing adequate yearly progress to the Department of Education. NCLB places particularly strong emphasis on reading and math by requiring states to assess students yearly from Grades 3 through 8 and once during high school. NCLB also requires states to assess their students in science at least once during each of three grade spans: Grades 3–5, 6–9, and 10–12.

An RTI framework, and specifically its focus on progress monitoring, provides a comprehensive approach to a school's ongoing efforts to help all students meet grade-level expectations. As states continue their assessment programs, they recognize the importance of monitoring student progress toward grade-level benchmarks prior to the yearly assessments. The alignment of progress monitoring measures with state assessments provides schools a way to target students who may be at risk for not achieving state-determined, grade-level standards. The progress monitoring component of RTI might also prove helpful in considering NCLB's safe harbor provision, which means that schools may meet adequate yearly progress if they can demonstrate that students are making progress toward proficiency (Nagle, Yunker, & Malmgren, 2006).

In summary, the intended goal of NCLB is to ensure high achievement for all students and to align curriculum, instruction, and assessment through its emphasis on scientifically based research and accountability. As noted, RTI has clear parallels to these goals with its own goals for high student achievement and the alignment of instruction, interventions, and assessment to promote student learning.

Key Elements of Reading First

Reading First is the part of NCLB that is dedicated to ensuring all children learn to read on grade level by the third grade. Reading First provides funding to states and many school districts to support high-quality reading programs based on the best scientific research. Consistent with findings from the National Reading Panel (National Institute of Child Health and Human Development, 2000), Reading First identifies five essential components of reading instruction: phonemic awareness, phonics, fluency, vocabulary, and comprehension. Reading First also emphasizes the need to select instructional and assessment tools and practices that have been determined to be effective with students at risk for early reading failure.

An important component of Reading First includes a provision to provide professional development for teachers of students in kindergarten through Grade 3 on effective reading instruction and assessment practices. In summary, building on the findings of the National Reading Panel, the program goals are to improve reading achievement by selecting, implementing, and providing professional development for teachers using scientifically based reading programs and by ensuring accountability through ongoing, valid, and reliable screening, diagnostic, and classroom-based assessment.

RTI presents an organizing framework through which schools can meet the requirements of Reading First and through which schools can promote higher student achievement in reading. Specifically, RTI incorporates screening and progress monitoring measures, early intervention for students learning to read, and evidence-based practices at all tiers of intervention.

Key Provisions of IDEA 2004

The Individuals with Disabilities Education Act (IDEA, 2004) is the federal legislation governing educational processes that serve people with disabilities from birth to age 21. The most recent changes in regulations emphasize the need to improve educational outcomes for students with disabilities by including them in accountability and assessment systems. Additionally, IDEA 2004 focuses on providing access to the general education curriculum for students with disabilities through the use of evidenced-based instructional practices. Other significant changes within the most recent IDEA regulations include the use of RTI as one way to identify specific learning disabilities and provide early intervening services for students who are determined to be at risk for learning problems.

A shift at the federal level toward achieving greater policy coherence is seen in the effort to align many of IDEA regulations with NCLB. Specifically, IDEA aligns with NCLB by ensuring that educational personnel are highly qualified, specifying that research-based interventions are used, enhancing student progress through the use of early intervening services, and preventing overidentification and disproportionate representation of minority students in special education. Similar to NCLB, IDEA also requires that states submit annual state performance plans to report progress and performance across indicators associated with specified monitoring priorities. More important, the state performance plan represents a useful tool for defining a problem, collecting and evaluating data, and making data-based decision plans for improvement at the state level.

Elements of IDEA that align with the RTI framework include scientifically based research, early intervening services, prevention of overidentification and disproportionate representation, and special requirements for determining and documenting the presence of a disability. At the student level, IDEA requires evidence that a student has had appropriate instructional opportunities in the general education classroom as part of a comprehensive evaluation for identification of learning disabilities. This evidence comes in the form of observation of the classroom environment and data collected on the student's progress within the general curriculum. Furthermore, students identified as having a disability and receiving services under IDEA must have an individualized education program (IEP) that includes present levels of performance in the relevant academic areas, annual goals, progress monitoring plans, and a description of the intervention and services needed. The IEP is agreed on by a collaborative team that uses existing information to guide its development.

In summary, IDEA focuses on improving educational outcomes for students with disabilities. Within IDEA, there is an increased emphasis on gaining access to the general curriculum through the use of scientifically based instruction and interventions, inclusion in assessment systems, and the use of routine progress monitoring. Specific regulations of IDEA 2004 allow for professional development for teachers to provide high-quality instructional and assessment practices that result in higher student achievement. Many of these changes in IDEA align with the RTI framework, including the focus on early intervention, data collection, and the use of evidence-based practices.

Table 2.1   Crosswalk of RTI, NCLB 2001, Reading First, and IDEA 2004

	RTI	*NCLB 2001*	*Reading First*	*IDEA 2004*
Statement of Purpose	Provides a schoolwide model of integrated instruction, assessment, and data-based decision making to improve student outcomes.	Requires that all students reach high standards in reading, writing, and math and graduate from high school.	Focuses on increased reading achievement for students in Grades K–3.	Improves educational outcomes for students with disabilities.
Instructional Program Coherence	Requires both horizontal and vertical alignment of instructional practices, screening, and monitoring.	Requires an integrated instruction and assessment system. Requires assessment of student progress in the state curriculum.	Requires the use of scientifically based instruction and assessment in the essential components of reading from Grades K–3, including supplemental support for students with reading difficulties.	Requires the use of research-based interventions, progress monitoring, accountability, and access to the general curriculum, as well as alignment of transition services with postschool opportunities.
Building Capacity	Focuses on schoolwide systems requires greater collaboration of teachers and staff to coordinate efforts of instructional delivery, assessment, and decision making.	Requires data collection and evaluation to determine adequate yearly progress. Requires that teachers be highly qualified.	Emphasizes capacity building through its focus on procuring instructional materials and providing professional development for K–3 teachers in the essential components of reading instruction.	Encourages capacity building through the inclusion of an early-intervening services provision that includes providing interventions to students at risk and related professional development for teachers.

Summary

Using the policy coherence framework as an organizing principle, Table 2.1 juxtaposes RTI, NCLB 2001, Reading First, and IDEA 2004.

As illustrated, these policy initiatives have much in common with the PLC and school improvement research. An RTI framework provides an increased level of precision to the process of increasing student achievement. Through its focus on increasing student achievement, aligning instruction and assessment practices, and data-based decision making at the schoolwide level, RTI is consistent with other best practice and federal policy initiatives that govern schools today, and therefore provides schools a model through which they can work toward greater policy coherence and IPC.

References

Ashby, D. E., Maki, D. M., & Cunningham-Morris, A. (1996, Winter). Organization development: Using data for decision making. *Journal of Staff Development, 17*(1), 8–11.

Astuto, T. A., Clark, D. L., Read, A-M., McGree, K., & Fernandez, L. de K. P. (1993). *Challenges to dominant assumptions controlling educational reform.* Andover, MA: Regional Laboratory for the Educational Improvement of the Northeast and Islands.

DuFour, R., & Eaker, R. E. (1998). *Professional learning communities at work: Best practices for enhancing student achievement.* Bloomington, IN: National Education Service.

Elementary and Secondary School Act. (1965). Public Law 89-10.

Gerber, M. (2005). Teachers are still the test: Limitations of response to instruction strategies for identifying children with learning disabilities. *Journal of Learning Disabilities, 38*(6), 516–524.

Goodlad, J. I., Mantle-Bromley, C., & Goodlad, S. J. (2004). *Education for everyone: Agenda for education in a democracy*, San Francisco: Jossey-Bass.

Herbert, K. S., Murphy, K. M., Ramos, M. A., Vaden-Kiernan, M., & Buttram, J. L. (2005). SEDL's working systemically model: Final report. Austin, TX: Southwest Educational Development Laboratory.

Honig, M. I., & Hatch, T. C. (2004). Policy coherence: How schools strategically manage multiple, external demands. *Educational Researcher, 33*(8), 16–30.

Hord, S. M. (1997). *Professional learning communities: Communities of continuous inquiry and improvement.* Austin, TX: Southwest Educational Development Laboratory.

Individuals with Disabilities Education Act of 2004 (IDEA). (2004). Public Law 108-446.

Nagle, K., Yunker, C., & Malmgren, K. W. (2006). Students with disabilities and accountability reform: Challenges identified at the state and local levels. *Journal of Disability Policy Studies, 17,* 28–39.

National Institute of Child Health and Human Development (NICHD). (2000). Report of the National Reading Panel. Teaching children to read: An evidence-based assessment of the scientific research literature on reading and its implications for reading instruction. NIH Publication No. 00–4769. Washington, DC: U.S. Government Printing Office.

Newmann, F. M., Smith, B. A., Allensworth, E., & Bryk, A. S. (2001). Instructional program coherence: What it is and why it should guide school improvement policy. *Educational Evaluation and Policy Analysis, 23*(4), 297–321.

No Child Left Behind Act (NCLB). (2001). Public Law 107-110.

Spillane, J. P., Reiser, B. J., & Reimer, T. (2002). Policy implementation and cognition: Reframing and refocusing implementation research. *Review of Educational Research, 72,* 387–431.

Stecker, P. M., Fuchs, L. S., & Fuchs, D. (2005). Using curriculum-based measurement to improve student achievement: Review of research. *Psychology in the Schools, 42*(8), 795–819.

Togneri, W., & Anderson, S. E. (2003). Beyond islands of excellence: what districts can do to improve instruction and achievement in all schools. Baltimore: Learning First Alliance.

3

Schoolwide Screening

Academic and behavioral screening is regarded as a central feature of early intervention. This chapter helps readers understand the value and distinctive features of screening. A number of alternative procedures and test instruments across content areas and grade levels are available for screening. The information provided in this chapter can be used to help school staffs make informed decisions about selecting and implementing screening instruments. In addition to providing definitions and descriptions of screening, we also provide implementation checklists and school-based examples of how screening functions within an RTI process.

Definitions and Features

What Is Screening?

An important first step in any prevention approach is school-wide screening of students to accurately identify those who are at risk for learning difficulties. Screening is a type of assessment characterized by quick, low-cost, repeatable testing of age-appropriate critical skills (e.g., identifying letters of the alphabet or reading a list of high-frequency words) or behaviors (e.g., tardiness, aggression, or hyperactivity).

The basic question for a screening measure is whether the student should be judged as "at risk" for the target behavior. An example of a well-known screening instrument is the Snellen eye chart (Snellen, 1862). Using that eye chart, the school nurse screens students for potential vision problems. A student who has difficulty reading the chart is referred for more in-depth assessment of the specific problems he appears to be experiencing. Similarly, students may be screened for academic problems in a specific academic area, such as reading. The screening in this case is used to determine which students are at risk for encountering difficulties in learning to read. Students identified as at risk for reading problems are then referred for a more in-depth assessment of their reading ability.

For a screening measure to be useful, the measure must achieve an appropriate balance of accuracy and efficiency (Jenkins, 2003). Each of these features is described in detail below.

Accuracy

The critical feature of a screening tool is its ability to accurately classify students as being at risk or not at risk. A perfect screen would have a 100% accurate classification rate, as depicted in Figure 3.1. In this figure, the screening tool has correctly identified students who are not at risk for reading failure and do not later develop reading problems. Additionally, students who are at risk and later develop problems have been accurately identified. Unfortunately, achieving perfect results with a screening tool is highly unlikely. Therefore, schools must consider accuracy in relation to the sensitivity and specificity of the measures. *Sensitivity* is a screening measure's ability to identify "true positives"; that is, those students who perform poorly on the screen and do have reading problems, and, therefore, will require more intense levels of instruction and intervention to learn to read well. *Specificity* refers to the screening measure's ability

Figure 3.1   The Ideal Screen

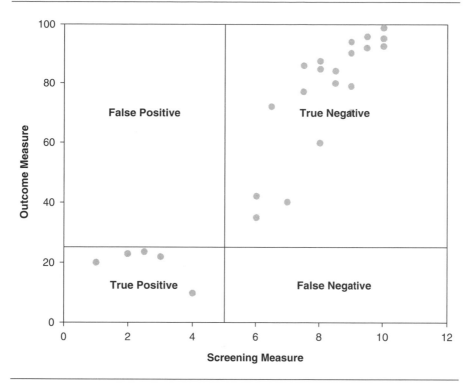

NOTE: Setting a cut score of 5 on the screening measure accurately discriminates between those at risk (true positive) and those not at risk (true negative).

to identify "true negatives"; that is, those students who do not perform poorly on the screen and do not have reading problems.

Because screening does not directly result in a diagnosis, it is better for a screening instrument to err on the side of false positives (identify students as at risk that might not be at risk). Therefore, a wider net with which to capture potentially at-risk students can be cast with screening measures. However, because identifying more students as at risk requires resources for further assessment and possibly intervention, schools need to maintain data on how well their screening measure identifies students as at risk. An example of a data chart that might be helpful in tracking the accuracy of screening measures is presented in Figure 3.2.

Factors that can affect a screening measure's sensitivity and specificity include whether the measure is criterion- or norm-referenced, and what cut scores distinguish levels of performance. (A *cut score* is the point that represents the dividing line between students who are not at risk and those who are potentially at risk.) Screening measures

Figure 3.2   School-Level Data Collection Sheet to Adjust Cut Scores

Student ID	Grade Level	Fall Screen Score	Winter Screen Score	Spring Screen Score	District Reading Assessment	Grade Point Average	State Reading Assessment

NOTE: Once data are entered, creating graphs that plot screening scores as the x (horizontal) axis and outcome scores as the y (vertical) axis will provide visual support for determining or adjusting cut scores and determining how well the screening measures are predicting later outcomes. Running correlational analyses of data also gives an estimate of the screen's predictive validity.

can use either a criterion- or a norm-referenced standard of performance. A *criterion-referenced measure* compares a student's performance to a predetermined performance level on a set of academic goals. An example of a criterion-referenced measure for reading might include a student reading a passage at grade level, with a goal of correctly reading a specified number of words a minute. Any student who fails to meet that measure would be considered at risk for reading problems. The important consideration in selecting a criterion-referenced measure is ensuring that it has strong predictive validity of a given academic skill (Jenkins, 2003). For example, how well does performance on oral reading fluency predict a student's overall reading ability? Maintaining data and conducting regression analyses can help schools answer this question and adjust their screening procedures accordingly. For instance, how well does the screen predict performance on the outcome?

A *norm-referenced measure* compares the screening results to an appropriate target group (e.g., other students the same grade). Students who fall within a predetermined percentile would be considered at risk for the relevant academic area. For example, if oral reading fluency is the measure, with a norm-referenced screen students whose score fell within the bottom 25% of all scores across the grade level might be identified as at risk for reading problems.

Criterion-referenced measures are preferred in the screening process because they give more accurate information about performance on relevant skills. In selecting a criterion-referenced measure, schools should attempt to link the measures at each grade level to existing performance measures, including performance standards in the school's curriculum (Jenkins, 2003). The content must be relevant to grade level and the skill in question (Jenkins).

Accuracy of screening is also determined by the cut scores that are used to distinguish students as being at risk or not at risk. Adjusting cut scores can affect the screening tool's sensitivity and specificity (Catts, 2006). Using the information collected in a data collection system such as the one presented in Figure 3.2, a school can plot performance on the screening measure with subsequent performance on the targeted skill. Figure 3.3 shows an example of the distribution of scores on a screening measure and subsequent performance on the state assessment. In this example, the outcome measure has a performance standard of 400 (e.g., students performing at or above this standard are considered proficient in the academic content or skill). As a result, students whose scores fall below that standard are considered to be not proficient. Figure 3.3 presents only one possible example of a cut score to identify students as at risk for not meeting standard on the outcome measure. Figure 3.4 shows the same distribution of scores; however, in this graph, the cut score has been adjusted, leading to changes in the sensitivity and specificity of the screening measure. The number of true positives and true negatives changed with the change in the cut score. True positives increased but the number of true negatives decreased. Also, the false positives increased and would be judged as at risk. The number of misses or false negatives decreased. School staff must weigh the consequences of such changes. Although many educators would agree it is better to identify more students as at risk, a negative consequence would be the strain on resources to provide intervention.

Efficiency

A second critical feature of a screening procedure is that it must be brief and easy to implement reliably (Jenkins, 2003). Although

Figure 3.3   Screening and Outcome Measures With Cut Scores

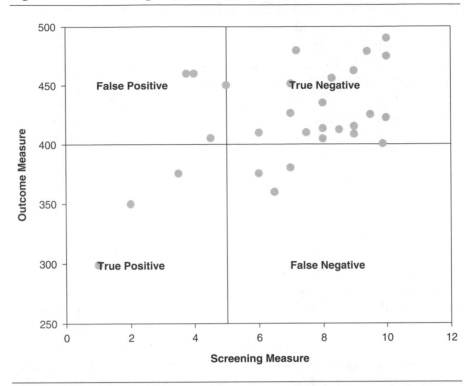

NOTE: Setting the cut score on the screening measure at 5 identifies six students as being at risk and places one student on the cut line. Three students identified as at risk have successful reading outcome measures. If we err on the side of caution and classify students on the screening cut score as at risk, this screening measure has sensitivity of 50% and specificity of 87%.

increasing the breadth and depth of a screening procedure can help improve its accuracy in correctly classifying students, schools must consider the cost benefit of such changes. For example, given the many components of reading (phonemic awareness, decoding, fluency, vocabulary, and comprehension), a screening procedure may encompass assessment of one, some, or all of these components to predict reading problems. Whereas a combination of measures may result in more accurate identification of students as being at risk or not being at risk, administering several measures to all students requires a significant increase in resources for screening. Conversely, identifying too many students as being at risk because a screening measure is brief, but not very accurate, requires a significant increase in resources for subsequent progress monitoring and intervention.

Research on screening for reading problems in early grades has demonstrated that a screening procedure that consists of the following

Figure 3.4   Changing the Cut Score Changes Who Is Judged as At Risk

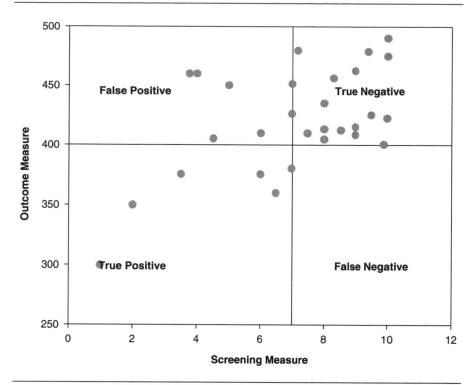

NOTE: If we err on the side of caution and identify students on the cut lines as at risk, increasing the cut score on the screening measure to 7 identifies 13 students as at risk. Seven students identified as at risk have successful reading outcomes. This screening measure has sensitivity of 100% and specificity of 70%.

reduces the number of false positives while maintaining an efficient screening procedure:

- Universal screening conducted three times over the school year
- Subsequent progress monitoring in Tier 1 for a period of five to six weeks for students identified as at risk by the screening measure (Compton, Fuchs, Fuchs, & Bryant, 2006)

Implementation

Implementing academic and behavioral screening poses several challenges, including administrative issues such as scheduling and record keeping. The greater challenges, however, are associated with ensuring

Table 3.1   Essential Task List for Screening

Directions

In the second column, *Responsible Person(s)*, write the name(s) of the individual or team who will assume responsibility for the task identified in the first column. In the third column, *Timeline/Status*, write the deadline for the task and/or the status of the task.

Task	Responsible Person(s)	Timeline/Status
Review your screening instrument's items to be certain that content is aligned with the curriculum for each grade level.		
Once a tool has been selected, determine and secure the resources required for implementation (e.g., computers, folders and copies, testing areas).		
Determine initial professional development needs and ongoing training support.		
Administer the screening measure three times a year (early fall, midterm, and late spring).		
Create a database that aligns with the screening instrument to hold student information and scores.		
Organize the screening results (e.g., graphs and tables) to provide a profile of all students and comparisons with each other.		
Monitor results at the classroom level and make decisions about when teachers or instructional programs require more scrutiny and support.		
Add screening results to a database so that students' performance can be monitored over time.		
Specify written steps to follow when further scrutiny is needed for students judged to be at risk.		

SOURCE: Mellard & McKnight, 2006.

that the staff has the knowledge to use the screening results in curricular decisions regarding their class and individual students. Screening measures can help inform instruction, but the measures themselves should not drive instruction. Table 3.1 identifies the essential tasks that school and district level staffs must consider to implement academic and behavioral screening.

What Is the Role of Screening Within an RTI model?

In the RTI model, proactive screening procedures are best used at least three times an academic year (at the beginning, middle, and end) and are used as general screening procedures for all students. Screening results can be used to target students who may be at risk by comparing their performance relative to a criterion or normative index of performance.

Screening is important because it represents the first gate or point of entry into subsequent tiers of RTI instruction (e.g., Tier 2, secondary interventions; and Tier 3, tertiary interventions). Screening is not a one-time event but rather is an iterative process taking place during the school year and across grade levels. During the course of general instruction (Tier 1), the school uses schoolwide screening in essential academic areas to identify each student's level of proficiency (usually three times a year). The screening data are organized to allow for comparison of both group (e.g., class) and individual performance. Comparisons of group performance can provide feedback about class performance to school leadership to identify when a teacher may require additional support, for example. Individual performance helps identify students who are potentially at risk for not acquiring the academic skill.

As mentioned, ideally, screening should be conducted at least three times a year. One-time screening at the beginning of the school year can overidentify students as at risk (Fuchs & Fuchs, 2006). That is, one-time screenings at the beginning of the school year yield more false positive errors than is generally acceptable. Research examining standards for screening suggests that one way to help make the screening process more efficient is to combine screening with five to six weeks of supplemental progress monitoring for students identified as at risk on the initial screen (Compton et al., 2006). The supplemental progress monitoring provides a way to reserve Tier 2 interventions for students who continue to show signs of being at risk for reading difficulties (Compton et al.).

Table 3.2   Standards for Judging High-Quality Screening

Directions

Read each of the standards that have been identified as mechanisms for judging high-quality screening. The checklist is formatted so that you can indicate current and planned implementation.

- If the practice has been implemented, indicate that with a checkmark (✓).
- If the practice is being developed, rank by priority. Indicate 1 = of highest priority through 3 = of lowest priority. (Thus, practices ranked as "1" would be implemented before those ranked as "2," and those ranked as "2" would be implemented before those ranked as "3.")

	Status	
Standard	*In Place* (✓)	*Priority* (1–2–3)
Screening is schoolwide, meets accepted psychometric standards,[1] and has evidence of documented reliability[2] and concurrent[3] and predictive[4] validity within the particular school setting.		
Individuals involved in the administration, scoring, and interpretation of the screening measures are appropriately trained.		
The site obtains screening data following a designated, fixed schedule.		
Data resulting from screening are documented and analyzed to refine the process.		
An established data-management system allows ready access to students' screening data.		
Cut scores are reviewed frequently and adjusted as necessary.		
A rationale is provided for the cut scores and decision rules (e.g., normative or specific criteria reference).		

NOTES

1. Psychometric standards are the theoretical approaches and procedures used to measure the difference between individuals' knowledge, attitudes, abilities, and personality traits.

2. Documented reliability is the extent to which a measurement yields consistent results over repeated testing of the same measure under identical conditions.

3. Concurrent validity occurs when a new measurement or test correlates well with a previously validated measure.

4. Predictive validity is the extent to which performance on one measure predicts performance on a later, related measure.

Standards for Judging High-Quality Screening

Screening tools must be aligned with the requirements of the school district, school site, and curriculum. The process outlined in this chapter can help a school develop screening measures that reach the optimal balance between accuracy and efficiency to correctly identify those students whose performance warrants intervention. Table 3.2 presents standards for judging high-quality screening that are based on the research in this area and that were used as part of a national effort to identify model RTI sites (Mellard, Byrd, Johnson, Tollefson, & Boesche, 2004).

Changing Structures and Roles

As with most elements within the RTI model, implementation of schoolwide screening procedures necessitates a closer collaboration among general education and specialist staff. Thus, when planning for the implementation of schoolwide screening, school leaders must include both the acquisition of resources and the time needed to administer screening. Schools must develop a standard procedure for identifying students as at risk. Additionally, the procedure will need to be adjusted based on existing data, so initial implementation also requires the development of a database that can accurately record screening, progress monitoring, and outcome data for students so that cut scores and criteria can be adjusted as necessary. This is an iterative, continual process. Table 3.3 divides school personnel into three areas and describes the responsibilities that personnel within these areas may be expected to undertake in schoolwide screening.

Challenges to Implementation

Universal screening in academic skills and behavior provides the information that determines which students enter Tier 2 in the RTI process and receive interventions (Fuchs & Fuchs, 2006). Therefore, accuracy of the screening measure is paramount. Additionally, because it is conducted schoolwide, screening needs to be efficient. As RTI moves to curricular areas beyond early reading, screening measures that have appropriate discriminant and predictive validity are required for areas such as math, writing, and, later, reading. Discriminant validity refers to the accuracy with which scores represent different knowledge, skills, and ability. For example, one would expect that reading and math scores reflect (discriminate) between students' knowledge in these two

Table 3.3   Changing Roles and Structures to Implement Screening

General Education

- Administer schoolwide screening measurements across content areas according to schedule.

- Administer assessments, and chart and evaluate results.

- Identify students for further monitoring.

- Provide information to parents if using the results for reporting student progress.

Specialist and Support Staff

- Assist general education teachers in implementation efforts.

- Collect data on a screening tool and associated cut scores to inform the process.

- Collaborate with the general education teacher to determine which students require further assessment.

Administration

- Lead effort to create infrastructure for schoolwide screening.

- Provide necessary technology, materials, and resources.

- Provide initial and continuing professional development opportunities for new staff and refresher training for incumbent staff.

- Ensure fidelity of implementation through routine, periodic observation, and discussions with staff.

- Research the availability of screening tool options with staff committee to select appropriate tools and methods.

- Incorporate this system so that it meets multiple requirements, including for example, determination of average yearly progress for the No Child Left Behind Act (NCLB, 2001), and ongoing progress monitoring.

- Determine if classroom performance warrants intervention (i.e., entire class performance is considerably lower than other classes in the same grade level).

- Review aggregate data of classrooms with teachers and district personnel to inform decision making.

NOTE: *General Education* includes the general education teacher. *Specialist and Support Staff* includes special education, reading or learning specialists, related services personnel, and paraprofessionals. *Administration* includes building principals and assistants, as well as curriculum and/or assessment specialists at building or district levels.

academic areas. Predictive validity refers to the accuracy with which a score is indicative of future performance. The higher the predictive validity, the more useful that test would be. For example, a kindergarten-level reading-screening test should be highly predictive of students' future reading ability. Below are some of the challenges that schools should prepare for when adopting universal screening measures:

1. *Logistical Issues of Administration.* School leaders must coordinate the necessary resources to conduct universal screening. Resources include having sufficient copies of the assessment instrument; scheduling, including make-up dates for absentees or missing data; scoring and analyzing results; and database development and maintenance.

2. *Distinguishing Screening From Progress Monitoring.* Although universal screening and progress monitoring use many of the same features, they are two distinct components of an RTI model. Screening measures are implemented to quickly identify students who may be at risk in the targeted academic area, whereas progress monitoring is a more complex assessment tool that determines both performance and growth in the relevant skill. Screening has a role in predicting future performance; progress monitoring focuses on accurately representing students' current learning and performance. Even though screening tools may be administered several times throughout the school year, performance on screening measures is not equivalent to progress monitoring in the general curriculum. Chapter 4 discusses progress monitoring in more detail.

3. *Selection of Screening Measures.* As noted earlier in this chapter, the ideal screening measure would accurately predict those students who are at risk from those students who are not at risk for future academic or behavioral difficulties. At best, however, screening tools are imperfect measures that indicate that a student requires in-depth assessment. The important considerations in selecting a screening measure include (a) predictive validity of the measure to the outcome, (b) discriminant validity of the measure and related cut scores, and (c) ease of implementation.

In elementary school–age students, the screening content usually focuses on the critical skills of reading, writing, and math that will assist in the acquisition of content knowledge (e.g., science, social studies, and language arts) at higher grade levels. For students in middle and high schools, the screening measures must also consider predicting behavioral outcomes such as dropping out of school. Such predictions can incorporate academic markers, but must also consider other indicators such as tardiness, absenteeism, and discipline referrals. These behavioral indicators become very important in decisions about interventions for older students.

4. *Determining Decision Rules.* The essential decision in the screening process is determining the criterion for classification. What is the cut score for determining risk? Some students will perform on the edge of the cut score, so guidelines must be established for determining when a particular student's performance warrants further investigation.

Screening in Practice

This section provides one school-based example of how screening occurs and how the results are used to inform decisions about curricular choices and students' tier placement.

Jefferson Elementary School, Pella, Iowa

Overview and Demographics

Jefferson Elementary School has a total enrollment of 500 students, with two sections each of kindergarten through third grade and six sections each of fourth and fifth grades. Nearly equal numbers of boys and girls attend the school. About 14% of the students (70) are eligible for free or reduced-cost lunch, and about 6.6% (33) receive special education services. Five percent (25) of the students are minority students, and the rest are Caucasian; 1.2% of the students (six) are English language learners.

Jefferson Elementary's RTI model consists of five tiers, in which the first four tiers represent interventions that become increasingly intense; the fifth tier is special education.

Screening for Reading Problems

Kindergarteners and first graders are screened using Dynamic Indicators of Basic Early Literacy Skills (DIBELS) (Kaminski & Good, 1998) assessments in the fall, winter, and spring. The school also uses DIBELS fluency and accuracy assessments for students in the second and third grades; and the Fuchs, Hamlett, and Fuchs (1997) fluency and accuracy assessments for students in the fourth and fifth grades. In addition to the fluency and accuracy measures, students in the second through fifth grades are assessed with the Iowa Test of Basic Skills in November, and the Gates-McGinitie (McGinitie, McGinitie, Maria,

Dreyer, & Hughes, 1999) in April. Second graders are also given the Gates-McGinitie in October.

Screening Data and Reference Points

When analyzing students' screening data, the school uses reference points, not specific cut scores. The reference points are used to indicate whether a student is performing below expectations and to guide school staff members as they determine appropriate interventions for students. The reference points, or scores, match up with proficiency scores of standardized tests.

No single score stands alone in determining interventions for students. Data from multiple sources are used to determine which students need instruction beyond Tier 1 and which interventions would be most effective in meeting student needs.

Analyzing Data

The literacy team, which includes general and special education teachers, reading intervention teachers, district staff, the curriculum director, and the principal, meets three times a year for Literacy Day sessions. These sessions, which occur just after districtwide student screenings, allow team members to review the districtwide screening data as well as data from the other schoolwide screening measures. Data are then used to make changes to student interventions and to identify students who require interventions that are more individualized and more intensive.

The team collects data on a "Literacy Day Data" sheet, which includes the names of the students in a class and scores earned by each of those students on fluency and accuracy measures, as well as the Gates-McGinitie comprehension and vocabulary tests. A companion sheet, "Literacy Day Notes," is used during meeting discussions to note a student's area of need, current intervention, and comments. An end result of the discussion is to make adjustments as needed based on student data. Students with skill deficits are considered for services, whereas students with extension needs are considered for gifted and talented placement.

Screening Challenges

Time is the biggest challenge. Staff members have trained a group of volunteers to administer fluency and accuracy screenings to reduce

(Continued)

(Continued)

the time teachers spend on assessments. They also have student interns from Central College to help administer, score, and record data.

Determining appropriate screening materials is another challenge. Finding screening measures to assess particular skills is difficult. Additionally, using multiple sources of data to inform the decision-making process takes organization, time, and careful analysis.

Finally, using the data to make appropriate decisions regarding interventions has been challenging for Jefferson Elementary staff. The data must be collected, recorded, and sorted in a way that facilitates analysis. At times, student screening data suggest the need for an intervention for which the school has no resources.

Summary

When RTI is implemented with fidelity and rigor, all students should benefit. An initial step in the RTI process is ensuring that students who are at risk for academic or behavioral difficulties are identified as early as possible. Early identification avoids the added complications students encounter through repeated failure, including negative changes in self-concept and efficacy. Schoolwide screening provides the initial closer examination at students' learning and performance, and those screening results can be used for indicating those students needing closer monitoring and more intense interventions and supports than are available in the Tier 1 of general education.

Resources

The following resources may support your implementation of universal screening efforts:

- **National Research Center on Learning Disabilities (http://www.nrcld.org)**

    The National Research Center on Learning Disabilities engages in research designed to help the learning disabilities field understand policies, practices, and prevalence of learning disability identification as well as to identify best practices. This site includes two helpful resources for screening: a paper written by Jenkins (2003), and a presentation by Catts (2006).

- **Edcheckup (http://www.edcheckup.com)**

  Offers an assessment system for screening student performance and measuring student progress toward goals in reading. This site offers a combination of free downloads and paid subscriptions that increase access to content.

- **EdProgress (http://www.edprogress.com)**

  EdProgress is a consulting company that focuses on assessment, large-scale testing and accountability, and systemic reform. With research-proven training materials, measurement tools, reporting systems, and teacher training interventions, EdProgress helps teachers become more focused on teaching and learning for all students.

- **Evidence-Based Progress Monitoring and Improvement System (http://www.aimsweb.com)**

  AIMSweb is a formative assessment system that informs the teaching and learning process by providing continuous student performance data and reporting improvement to students, parents, teachers, and administrators that enable evidence-based evaluation and data-driven instruction. Browsers must pay to view materials from the site.

- **Intervention Central (http://www.interventioncentral.org)**

  This site offers free tools and resources to help school staff and parents to promote positive classroom behaviors and foster effective learning for all children and youth. The site was created by Jim Wright, a school psychologist from Syracuse, NY. Materials on the site are free.

- **Monitoring Basic Skills Progress (http://www.proedinc .com/Scripts/prodView.asp?idProduct=1348)**

  Developed by Lynn Fuchs, Carol Hamlett, and Douglas Fuchs, Monitoring Basic Skills Progress is a computer program

(Continued)

(Continued)

for conducting automatic curriculum-based measurement and for monitoring student progress in reading, math computation, and math concepts and applications. The computer program will provide immediate feedback to students on their progress, and provide individual and classwide reports to teachers to help them plan more effective instruction. Browsers must order and pay for materials from this site.

- **National Center on Student Progress Monitoring (http://www.studentprogress.org)**

  The Center's mission is to provide technical assistance to states and districts and disseminate information about progress monitoring practices proven to work in different academic content areas (Grades K–5). Materials on this site are free.

- **Reading Success Lab (http://www.readingsuccesslab.com)**

  The Reading Success Lab provides software solutions to identify reading problems and improve reading skills. Some screening materials on the site are free, but browsers must order and pay for other materials.

References

Catts, H. W. (2006, April). Schoolwide screening. Presentation at the national SEA conference on responsiveness to intervention: Integrating RTI within the SLD [specific learning disability] determination process. Kansas City, MO. Retrieved July 12, 2006, from http://www.nrcld.org/sea/presentations_worksheets/screening/Catts_screening.pdf.

Compton, D. L., Fuchs, D., Fuchs, L. S., & Bryant, J. D. (2006). Selecting at-risk readers in first grade for early intervention: A two-year longitudinal study of decision rules and procedures. *Journal of Educational Psychology*, *98*, 394–409.

Fuchs, L. S., & Fuchs, D. (2006). Implementing responsiveness-to-intervention to identify learning disabilities. *Perspectives on Dyslexia*, *32*(1), 39–43.

Fuchs, L. S., Hamlett, C., & Fuchs, D. (1997). *Monitoring basic skills progress.* Austin, TX: Pro-Ed.

Jenkins, J. R. (2003, December). *Candidate measures for screening at-risk students*. Paper presented at the NRCLD responsiveness-to-intervention symposium, Kansas City, MO. Retrieved April 3, 2006, from http://www.nrcld.org/symposium2003/jenkins/index.html.

Kaminski, R. A., & Good, R. A. (1998). Use of curriculum-based measurement to assess early literacy: Dynamic indicators of basic early literacy skills. In M. R. Shinn (Ed.), *Advances in curriculum-based measurements and its use in a problem-solving model* (pp. 113–142). New York: Guilford.

MacGinitie, W. H., MacGinitie, R. K., Maria, K., Dreyer, L. G., & Hughes, K. E. (1999). *Gates-MacGinitie reading tests* (4th ed.). Rolling Meadows, IL: Riverside.

Mellard, D., Byrd, S., Johnson, E., Tollefson, J., & Boesche, L. (2004). Foundations and research on identifying model responsiveness to intervention sites. *Learning Disability Quarterly, 27,* 243–256.

Mellard, D. F., & McKnight, M. A. (2006). RTI implementation tool for reading: Best practices [Brochure]. Lawrence, KS: National Resource Center on Learning Disabilities.

No Child Left Behind Act (NCLB). (2001). Public Law 107-110.

Snellen, H. (1862). *Scala tipografia measurae il visus.* Utrecht, Netherlands.

4

Progress Monitoring

In order to know if students are benefiting from instruction, teachers must routinely collect and analyze evidence of their performance. The data collected as part of this process help to inform subsequent instructional decisions at both the classroom and the individual levels. For example, if many children in a classroom are not performing to benchmark standards, this may be an indication that the curriculum or instruction, or both, should be reviewed. If an individual student is not performing to standard, careful monitoring of that student's progress can help teachers devise effective interventions to support her learning. Frequent assessments of the relevant skill provide data on which to base decisions, such as changing the instructional program or referring a student to another tier of intervention. This systematic process, known as progress monitoring, lies at the heart of the RTI model.

Chapter at a Glance

Definitions and Features

What Is Progress Monitoring?

Progress monitoring is the scientifically based practice of assessing students' academic performance on a regular basis for two purposes: (1) to determine whether students are benefiting appropriately from the instructional program, and (2) to build more effective programs for the children who are not benefiting appropriately (Fuchs & Fuchs, n.d.). In an RTI paradigm, progress monitoring assists school teams in making decisions about which level of intervention is most appropriate (National Center on Student Progress Monitoring, 2006). Progress monitoring is a valid and efficient tool for gauging the effectiveness of instruction and providing important information for eventual classification and placement decisions (Stecker, Fuchs, & Fuchs, 2005).

Several types of assessments can provide information on the status of students' knowledge, skills, and abilities. While practitioners sometimes interchange various progress monitoring procedures with schoolwide screening and diagnostic tests, it is important to differentiate among these kinds of assessments. Table 4.1 highlights several distinguishing purposes of these three assessments.

In order for progress monitoring to be useful within an RTI context, it should include the following features:

1. The monitoring should occur in all tiers of intervention.

2. The measures should be directly related to the curriculum, grade level, and tier level.

3. The assessments should be easy and efficient to administer. (Many computer-based options exist to ease implementation; see the Resources section, this chapter.)

4. The results should be displayed in ways that make analysis and evaluation efficient. (Line graphs that depict progress are commonly used and provide a visual display of student progress.)

5. Cut scores and decision rules for the level, slope, or percentage of mastery must be designated to help determine if a student is responding adequately.

6. A rationale must be provided for the cut scores and decision rules.

7. The measures should be administered frequently to inform instruction and curricular placement decisions (guidelines for frequency are given in each tier).

8. A student's performance on the measures should represent *one* source for informing the development of instructional strategies.

Table 4.1   Purposes of Three Types of Assessment

	Screening	*Progress Monitoring*	*Diagnostic*
Focus	Schoolwide	Class Small group Student	Individual student
Academic Target	Broad index	Specific academic skill or behavioral target	Specific academic domains
Frequency of Administration	Yearly Three times a year	Weekly Three times or more each week Daily	Yearly
Purpose	Identification of students at risk	Instructional decisions (class or individual)	Identification of specific student deficits
Level of Information	Class or school instruction and curriculum decisions	Within intervention (curriculum/ instruction)	Selection of curriculum and instructional methods
Implications	First step of intervention planning	Continue or revise placement	Planning or specifying intervention

Implementation

What Is the Role of Progress Monitoring Within an RTI Model?

Progress monitoring serves an important function in an RTI model, especially when RTI is used as a gateway to specific learning disabilities (SLDs) determination. Research has documented that teachers who routinely measure student progress, analyze the results, and adjust their instructional practice accordingly have higher student achievement than those who do not (Fuchs, 1989; Stecker et al., 2005). Progress monitoring essentially provides the indication of the "response" within an RTI framework. If applied with rigor, progress monitoring helps a school identify students who require additional interventions and helps determine whether a given intervention is successful. Furthermore, as part of disability determination, the results of progress monitoring address the federal legal stipulation that students who are determined as having a disability have not benefited from general education instruction. Within an RTI model, progress monitoring serves various functions at each tier, as illustrated below.

Progress Monitoring in Tier 1

Progress monitoring is used in Tier 1 for the following:

1. It is used to determine whether a student is making sufficient progress in the general curriculum.

2. At the school level, progress monitoring provides a classroom-by-classroom measure of student progress.

3. For students who have "exited" from a higher level of intervention, progress monitoring provides continued monitoring to determine if they are making sufficient progress.

Progress Monitoring Versus General Screening

In Chapter 3, we described the process of schoolwide screening. Progress monitoring differs from screening in important ways, including the frequency with which it is administered and the kind of information it provides about student performance. Proactive screening procedures are best used at least three times a year and are used as general screening procedures for all students. Screening targets students who may be at risk by comparing their performance to a criterion-referenced measure. Progress monitoring, on the other hand, provides routine data that display student growth over time to determine if a student is progressing as expected in the curriculum. The research suggests that, ideally, progress monitoring should consist of weekly measures that are routinely reviewed and analyzed by the classroom teacher (Stecker et al., 2005). When students fail to make adequate progress, it is an indication that an instructional change is required.

Curriculum-Based Measurement

Curriculum-based measurement (CBM) is one option for monitoring progress. CBM assesses the different skills covered in the annual curriculum by providing equivalent alternate forms (Deno, 2003). For example, in September, a CBM math test assesses all the math skills to be covered during the entire year (Fuchs et al., 1994). In November, February, and May, the weekly CBM tests the annual curriculum in exactly the same way but with different items (Fuchs et al.). Therefore, scores earned at different times during the school year may be compared to determine whether a student's performance is increasing, decreasing, or staying the same (National Center on Student Progress Monitoring, 2006).

CBM is used in progress monitoring because with equivalent assessments, it is much easier to discern student growth (Deno, 2003). In this way, as part of a progress monitoring system, CBM is superior to a mastery-of-skills approach (e.g., end-of-unit tests that focus only on a particular component of the curriculum) because CBM shows if students are maintaining the range of skills and provides a general indication of performance and growth (Deno).

Computer-based examples of CBM for reading and math include

- Monitoring basic skills progress (Pro-Ed Online, 2006)
- Dynamic Indicators of Basic Early Literacy Skills (DIBELS, 2006)
- Intervention CBM probes (Intervention Central, 2006)

How Progress Monitoring Informs Instruction

The results of progress monitoring in Tier 1 inform decision making about classroom instruction in two main ways (Fuchs & Fuchs, n.d.):

1. At the class level, the average performance of the class and their rate of growth can help a teacher or administrator determine how to create instructional and curricular change so that

all students reach proficiency on a given skill. For example, the chart in Figure 4.1 shows the oral reading fluency (ORF) levels of all students in a classroom. Based on published norms (Hasbrouck & Tindal, 2005), second-grade reading fluency ranges from 11 words a minute to about 106 words a minute. As a result, students reading 25 words or fewer a minute fall below the 25th percentile. This chart shows that Mary, Lucas, and Mimi are struggling, whereas the majority of the class is performing at the 50th percentile or better.

2. At the individual student level, schools use predetermined cut scores (level) and rates of progress (slope) to identify students in need of more extensive and intensive interventions in Tier 2. Based on the example in Figure 4.1, Mary, Lucas, and Mimi would require more frequent progress monitoring. An individual chart for Mary is presented in Figure 4.2. Based on published norms for growth (Hasbrouck & Tindal, 2005), Mary is not making adequate progress in Tier 1, and therefore should be considered for placement in Tier 2.

Figure 4.1   Classroom Progress Monitoring Data

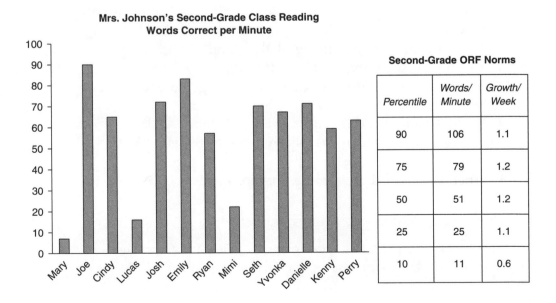

SOURCE: Hasbrouck & Tindal (2005).

Figure 4.2   Mary's Individual Progress

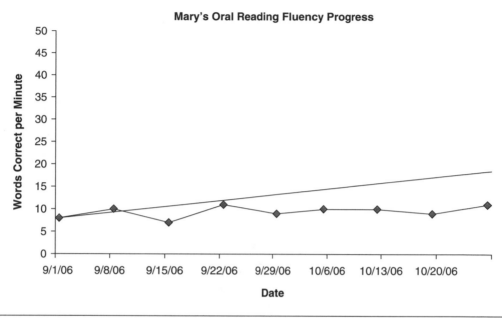

Progress Monitoring in Tier 2

In Tier 2, the purpose of progress monitoring shifts slightly. The main purpose of progress monitoring here is to determine whether an intervention is successful in helping the student learn at an appropriate rate. Decision rules need to be created to determine the following:

1. When a student might no longer require Tier 2 services and can be returned to the general classroom (Tier 1)

2. When the intervention needs to be changed

3. When a student might be identified for special education

Because timely decisions about student progress at this tier are critical for the student's long-term achievement, research-based recommendations (Stecker et al., 2005) are to do the following:

1. Assess student progress using CBM in Tier 2 twice a week

2. Chart these results and analyze student progress regularly

3. Use preset rules to determine when a student is not adequately responding to an intervention (commonly suggested rules are that three consecutive data points below the goal line warrant changes to the intervention) (Fuchs, 1989; National Association of State Directors of Special Education, 2005)

The textbox "Progress Monitoring for Tier 2" provides an example of progress monitoring of reading performance at Tier 2. Note the use of consistent and predetermined decision rules for instructional decision making.

Progress Monitoring for Tier 2

To monitor the progress of students receiving Tier 2 interventions, the staff at Dalton Gardens Elementary School administer DIBELS and Read Naturally fluency and comprehension probes weekly (Kaminski & Good, 1998). The DIBELS assessments include the following:

1. *First Grade.* Letter-naming fluency, phoneme segmentation fluency, nonsense word fluency, and ORF.

2. *Second Grade.* Nonsense word fluency and ORF.

3. *Third Through Fifth Grade.* ORF.

If a student has three data points that are above the aim line, the goal is increased until the student is performing at grade-level benchmarks. If a student has three data points below the goal line, the intervention is modified to better meet the student's needs. If, after the modification, the student again has three points below the aim line, the student is considered for Tier 3 intervention.

Progress Monitoring in Special Education

In special education, progress monitoring serves yet other purposes. First, the progress monitoring done to this point provides systematic, reliable, and multiple data points that should inform the eligibility determination decision and development of specially designed instruction to meet the student's individual needs. These data provide a good indication of a student's exposure to appropriate learning experiences, as required by IDEA 2004. Second, progress monitoring is a requirement of the individualized education program, and provides information about student progress toward short-term objectives and annual goals. The routine and frequent monitoring of student progress toward individualized education program goals has been shown to result in higher outcomes for students receiving special education services (Stecker et al., 2005).

Essential Task List for Implementation

Table 4.2 provides an essential task list for implementation of progress monitoring. While not exhaustive, the list represents important steps in initial implementation. The first column describes the specific task to be performed. The second column asks you to identify, by name, who has overall responsibility for overseeing this task. In some cases, more than one individual may be responsible. The final column allows you to either set target dates for completion or to indicate the status of progress related to the task.

Standards for Judging High-Quality Progress Monitoring

Progress monitoring tools must be aligned with the requirements of the district, school, and curriculum. Therefore, we do not make any recommendations on specific programs. However, regardless of the tools selected to implement and operate a system of progress monitoring, several criteria may be used to judge the quality of the system. Table 4.3 presents standards for judging high-quality progress monitoring that are based on the research in this area and that were used as part of a national effort to identify model RTI sites (Mellard, Byrd, Johnson, Tollefson & Boesche, 2004). The checklist is formatted so that you can indicate current and planned implementation. If a practice has been implemented, indicate so with a checkmark (✓). If the practice is being developed, rank its priority of focus: 1 = highest priority, 3 = lowest priority.

Table 4.2   Essential Task List for Progress Monitoring

Directions

In the second column, *Responsible Person(s),* write the name(s) of the individual or team who will assume responsibility for the task identified in the first column. In the third column, *Timeline/Status,* write the deadline for the task and/or status of the task.

Task	Responsible Person(s)	Timeline/Status
Tier 1		
Within the relevant content area, review the progress monitoring measure or tool selected for Tier 1 to determine if the content of the measure or tool is aligned with the school's curriculum.		
Once a tool has been selected, determine and secure the resources required to implement (e.g., computers, folders and copies, testing areas)		
Determine initial professional development needs and ongoing training support.		
Administer the screening measure frequently enough to assess a learner's responsiveness. At Tier 1, screening is three times a year, with routine monitoring on a weekly or biweekly basis.		
Monitor results at the individual student level and make decisions about reasonable cut scores to determine movement to Tier 2.		
Monitor results at the classroom level, and make decisions about when teachers or instructional programs require more scrutiny and support.		
Tier 2		
Within the relevant area of focus for the intervention, review the progress monitoring measure or tool selected for Tier 2 to determine if the content of the tool is aligned with the intervention.		

Task	Responsible Person(s)	Timeline/Status
Administer the progress monitoring measure frequently enough to assess a learner's responsiveness. At Tier 2, the research-based recommendation is two to five times per week.		
Organize results to provide a profile of the student's progress within this tier. This could be a graph of test scores supplemented with student work samples.		
Monitor results to determine if a student is responding to the intervention.		
Develop decision rules about when to return a student to Tier 1, when to continue with Tier 2, and if further scrutiny of student performance for special education is warranted.		
Special Education		
Develop a system to include progress monitoring records from Tier 1 and Tier 2 in special education evaluation or eligibility decisions.		
Ensure the special education teacher receives progress monitoring results on the individual student along with evidence gathered during eligibility process.		
Develop progress monitoring measures that are aligned with the student's annual goals and short-term objectives and that are included on the student's individualized education program.		
Administer the measure frequently enough to assess a learner's responsiveness.		

Table 4.3   Standards for Judging High-Quality Progress Monitoring

Directions

Read each of the standards that have been identified as mechanisms for judging high-quality progress monitoring. The checklist is formatted so that you can indicate current and planned implementation.

- If the practice has been implemented, indicate that with a checkmark (✓).
- If the practice is being developed, rank by priority. Indicate 1 = of highest priority through 3 = of lowest priority. (Thus, practices ranked as "1" would be implemented before those ranked as "2" and those ranked as "2" would be implemented before those ranked as "3.")

	Status	
Standard	*In Place (✓)*	*Priority (1–2–3)*
Scientific, research-based instruction includes continuous progress monitoring of student performance across all tiers.		
Teachers follow a designated procedure and schedule for progress monitoring and for regrouping students as needed.		
Measures are administered frequently to inform instruction and curricular placement decisions (i.e., in Tier 1, at least every three weeks; in Tier 2, one to two times a week; in special education, three to five times a week).		
Progress monitoring occurs in all tiers (including general education).		
Progress monitoring measures are appropriate to the curriculum, grade level, and tier level.		
Data resulting from progress monitoring are documented and analyzed.		
Progress monitoring uses a standardized benchmark by which progress is measured and determined to be either sufficient or insufficient.		
Teachers use progress monitoring data to evaluate instructional effectiveness and to be informed about the potential necessity for changing the instruction.		
An established data-management system allows ready access to students' progress monitoring data.		
After progress monitoring, a graph is completed to display data for analysis and decision making and to indicate the percentages of students who are at great risk, at some risk, and at low risk.		
Staff members receive training in the administration and interpretation of progress monitoring measures.		
The school designates reasonable cut scores and decision rules for the level, slope, or percentage of mastery to help determine responsiveness and distinguish adequate from inadequate responsiveness.		
Cut scores are reviewed frequently and adjusted as necessary.		
A rationale is provided for the cut scores and decision rules (e.g., normative or specific criteria reference).		

SOURCE: Mellard & McKnight (2006).

Changing Structures and Roles

School Structural Changes

Ideally, progress monitoring systems are consistent across the school. That is, although grade-level assessments will differ, the school must have an established data-management system that provides consistent and ready access to students' progress monitoring data. Consistency across grade levels facilitates communication among teachers and parents about a student's progress throughout her school career and provides accountability at the building level.

Building administrators, as well as both general and special education teachers must consider, create, and select appropriate assessments for use within a progress monitoring system. Such assessments must be consistent across classrooms at a particular grade level and similar in structure across grade levels but increasingly difficult as appropriate for a given grade level. The relationship between these tools and school content and performance standards must be considered. It is important to determine how progress monitoring tools inform student progress relative to a district's or state's performance benchmarks. One way to do this is to analyze student performance relative to performance on state and district assessments by including results on these performance measures in the database.

Because best practice suggests that progress monitoring be conducted on a weekly basis (Stecker et al., 2005), teachers and schools must develop the infrastructure to do so. A process for analyzing results at both the classroom level (to determine individual student performance) and the school level (to determine classroom performance) also must be developed and planned.

Table 4.4 lists potential changes to different roles and areas of school functioning under progress monitoring.

Impact on Conceptualizations of SLDs

Under a system of progress monitoring, SLD is primarily regarded as low achievement relative to classroom-peer functioning. If, for example, the bottom 25% of the class is selected for further progress monitoring or for placement in secondary interventions, a student's designation for Tier 2 intervention could vary depending on what class she is in. The use of a dual-discrepancy model to identify students whose performance is low and who have low rates of progress can help remove some of this variability. Continued progress monitoring is required through the tiers to be sure that students are responsive to all

Table 4.4   Changing Roles and Structures Under Progress Monitoring

---

General Education

- Implement the system of progress monitoring across content (reading, writing, math) areas.
- Administer assessments every three weeks or more frequently; chart and evaluate results.
- Identify students for diagnostic testing or for secondary intervention.
- Provide aggregate data of classroom results to principal.
- Provide information to parents if using the results for reporting student progress.
- Collaborate in selecting or creating progress monitoring tools.

Specialist and Support Staff

- Monitor progress of students in secondary or tertiary tiers of intervention in a particular content area.
- Administer relevant assessments; chart and evaluate results.
- Identify when a student is making adequate progress in a more intense instructional level.
- Collaborate with the general education teacher to assist in determination of students for secondary or tertiary tier intervention and to provide suggestions or consultation on instructional strategies for students.
- Incorporate progress monitoring goals into individualized education program development.

Administration

- Lead effort to create infrastructure for progress monitoring.
- Provide necessary technology, materials, and resources.
- Provide initial and continuing professional development opportunities for new staff and refresher training for incumbent staff.
- Ensure fidelity of implementation through routine, periodic observation and discussions with staff.
- Research the availability of CBM options with staff committee to select appropriate tools and methods.
- Incorporate this system so that it meets multiple requirements, including determination of average yearly progress for the No Child Left Behind Act (NCLB, 2001).
- Determine if classroom performance warrants intervention (i.e., entire class performance is considerably lower than other classes in the same grade level).
- Review aggregate data of classrooms and provide feedback to teachers.

NOTE: *General Education* includes the general education teacher. *Specialist and Support Staff* includes special education, reading or learning specialists, related services personnel, and paraprofessionals. *Administration* includes building principals and assistants, as well as curriculum and/or assessment specialists at building or district levels.

tiers of instruction. If a student responds (or makes progress) in secondary or tertiary levels of intervention, the team must decide whether progress is significant enough to warrant the student returning to Tier 1 (general education class), or whether the student should remain in the more-intense instruction to maintain levels of performance comparable to her peers. Some students identified as needing secondary or tertiary interventions may require more in-depth assessment to determine appropriate instructional interventions.

Teacher Training Issues

Initial training requirements will include orienting teachers toward the individual assessments and recording of information. Many teachers may be familiar with the concepts or be able to quickly learn and implement them after professional development opportunities. Many of the resources listed at the end of this chapter include detailed guides on implementation and recording of data that may be helpful in structuring such training sessions. Teachers also need to learn to analyze results to determine who will be identified for the next tier of intervention and when such intervention should take place. Analysis of results also needs to focus on interpretation to inform instructional strategies. That is, how can a student's performance on progress monitoring measures inform what occurs in the classroom? Based on a student's performance, what would constitute a reasonable instructional change? These areas will require more intense training in the relevant content areas. For example, teachers need to be well versed in theories and research on reading in order to determine the particular difficulty a student presents.

Ongoing training efforts include initial training for new teachers. In general, implementation-related issues will be the key to developing an ongoing training system. Using the standards for judging high-quality progress monitoring (see Table 4.3) as a starting point can help determine areas that require more training focus in a school. See the Resource section for Web sites, published software, and texts relevant to providing professional development.

Challenges to Implementation

An enormous growth in research, training, and implementation of progress monitoring and CBM has taken place (see, for example, http://www.studentprogress.org and http://progressmonitoring.net), and numerous resources exist to facilitate adoption, implementation, and maintenance. Nevertheless, schools will inevitably face challenges to implementation. An awareness of these challenges may help in developing workable solutions within the school and district context. Some challenges include the following:

1. *Selecting Appropriate Tools.* Although numerous systems exist (see the Resources section, below), it is important for schools and districts to select progress monitoring tools that fit the needs of their curriculum and that can be aligned with their district and state content and performance benchmarks.

2. *Limited Availability of Tools.* Currently, most CBM and other progress monitoring information is related to early reading, math, and, to a lesser extent, writing. Furthermore, there is no strong research base on progress monitoring for older students, and to date virtually no published programs target Grades 6 through 12.

3. *General Education Implementation.* Progress monitoring presents a paradigm shift for many teachers. Even when tools are available to facilitate the collection of data, a key to successful progress monitoring is for teachers to routinely, systematically, and thoughtfully analyze the data and make subsequent instructional decisions.

4. *"Bounce" in Measures.* Progress monitoring tools are general measures related to a specific content area. In reading, for example, a common progress monitoring assessment is a student's ORF, measured by timed readings on grade-level passages. Student performance on these measures can be affected by many factors, including familiarity with the content and background knowledge of the specific passage. Student performance on these measures often "bounces," providing inconsistent snapshots of a student's reading ability.

5. *Determining Decision Rules.* Progress monitoring is an overall check on a student's progression through the curriculum. In order for the system to be effective, several decision rules must be established. These include decision rules for the following:
   a. Establishing baselines. (How many data points will be needed?)
   b. Establishing high but reasonable goals. (How much progress can we expect?)
   c. Deciding when to make an instructional change. (Guidelines on this vary from 3 to 6 data points below the progress line.)
   d. Deciding when to consider movement to another tier of intervention (either up or down).
   e. Deciding when to consider referral to special education.

Progress Monitoring in Practice

The following example describes how Tualatin Elementary School, in Tualatin, Oregon, uses a schoolwide system of progress monitoring to inform its instructional decision making.

Decisions about future instruction are based on comparing progress monitoring results to predetermined decision rules. Decision rules include the following:

1. If fewer than 80% of the students in the general classroom are meeting benchmarks, staff reviews the core programs or implementation, or both, of instruction (Tier 1).

2. If students are below the 20th percentile in academic skills, they are placed in small-group instruction (Tier 2).

3. When progress data are below the aim line on three consecutive days, or when six data points produce a flat or decreasing trend line, school staff change the intervention.

4. When a student fails to progress after two consecutive small-group interventions, individual instruction begins (Tier 3).

5. When a student fails to progress after two consecutive individually designed interventions, the student is referred for special education evaluation.

Summary

Successful implementation of RTI relies heavily on systematic progress monitoring. Progress monitoring is an assessment process that informs instructional decision making. Within an RTI model, the types of decisions that a system of progress monitoring can inform include whether a student is making adequate progress in the general classroom, whether a student requires a more intensive level of intervention, and whether a student has responded successfully to an intervention and, therefore, can be returned to the general classroom.

Progress monitoring is closely related to other important concepts in the effective school literature, including data-based decision making, assessment for learning, and the professional teaching and learning cycle (DuFour & Eaker, 1998; Hord, 1997). Progress monitoring can best be conceptualized as a systematic, continuous, classroom-level assessment process. Achievement targets for each grade are defined, measures that reliably and validly assess those targets are selected, these measures are administered frequently, results are analyzed for performance and growth, and instructional decisions based on the results are made. At that point, the process begins again.

Resources

The following resources may support your implementation of progress monitoring.

- **Edcheckup (http://www.edcheckup.com)**

    This site offers an assessment system for screening student performance and measuring student progress toward goals in reading. The site offers a combination of free downloads and paid subscriptions that increase access to content.

- **EdProgress (http://www.edprogress.com)**

    This consulting company focuses on assessment, large-scale testing and accountability, and systemic reform. With research-proven training materials, measurement tools, reporting systems, and teacher training interventions, EdProgress helps teachers become more focused on teaching and learning for all students.

- **Evidence-Based Progress Monitoring and Improvement System (http://www.aimsweb.com)**

    AIMSweb is a formative assessment system that informs the teaching and learning process by providing continuous student performance data and reporting improvement to students, parents, teachers, and administrators to enable evidence-based evaluation and data-driven instruction. Browsers must pay to view materials from this site.

- **Intervention Central (http://www.interventioncentral.org)**

    This site offers free tools and resources to help school staff and parents to promote positive classroom behaviors and foster effective learning for all children and youth. The site was created by Jim Wright, a school psychologist from Syracuse, New York. Materials on this site are free.

- **Monitoring Basic Skills Progress (http://www.proedinc.com/Scripts/ prodView.asp?idProduct=1348)**

  Developed by Lynn Fuchs, Carol Hamlett, and Douglas Fuchs, Monitoring Basic Skills Progress is a computer program for conducting automatic CBM and for monitoring student progress in reading, math computation, and math concepts and applications. The computer program provides immediate feedback to students on their progress and provides individual and classwide reports to teachers to help them plan more effective instruction. Browsers must order and pay for materials from this site.

- **National Center on Accessing the General Curriculum (http://www.cast.org/ncac/ Curriculum-BasedEvaluations2913.cfm)**

  This link goes directly to an article titled "Curriculum-based evaluations," by Tracey Hall, PhD, Senior Research Scientist, National Center on Accessing the General Curriculum, and Missy Mengel, RA. It contains links to several Web sites related to progress monitoring.

- **National Center on Student Progress Monitoring (http://www.studentprogress.org)**

  The Center's mission is to provide technical assistance to states and districts and to disseminate information about progress monitoring practices proven to work in different academic content areas (Grades K–5). Materials on this site are free.

References

Deno, S. L. (2003). Developments in curriculum-based measurement. *Journal of Special Education, 37*(3), 184–192.

DuFour, R., & Eaker, R. E. (1998). *Professional learning communities at work: Best practices for enhancing student achievement.* Bloomington, IN: National Education Service.

Dynamic Indicators of Basic Early Literacy Skills (DIBELS). (2006). Retrieved March 9, 2006, from http://dibels.uoregon.edu.

Fuchs, L. S. (1989). Evaluating solutions: Monitoring progress and revising intervention plans. In M. R. Shinn (Ed.), *Curriculum-based measurement: Assessing special children* (pp. 153–181). New York: Guilford.

Fuchs, L. S., & Fuchs, D. (n.d.). What is scientifically based research on progress monitoring? Retrieved December 6, 2006, from http://www .studentprogress.org/library/What_is_Scientificall_%20Based_Research .pdf.

Fuchs, L. S., Fuchs, D., Hamlett, C. L., Thompson, A., Roberts, P. H., Kubec, P., & Stecker, P. M. (1994). Technical features of a mathematics concepts and applications curriculum-based measurement system. *Diagnostique, 19*(4), 23–49.

Hasbrouck, J. & Tindal, G. (2005). *Oral reading fluency: 90 years of measurement.* Retrieved November 30, 2006, from http:// brt.uoregon.edu/tech_ reports.htm.

Hord, S. M. (1997). *Professional learning communities: Communities of continuous inquiry and improvement.* Austin, TX: Southwest Educational Development Laboratory.

Individuals with Disabilities Education Act of 2004 (IDEA). (2004). Public Law 108-446.

Intervention Central. (2006). *Curriculum-based Measurement Warehouse.* Retrieved March 9, 2006, from http://www.interventioncentral.org.

Kaminski, R. A., & Good, R. A. (1998). Use of curriculum-based measurement to assess early literacy: Dynamic indicators of basic early literacy skills. In M. R. Shinn (Ed.), *Advances in curriculum-based measurements and its use in a problem-solving model* (pp. 113–142). New York: Guilford.

Mellard, D. F., & McKnight, M. A. (2006). RTI implementation tool for reading: Best practices [Brochure]. Lawrence, KS: National Resource Center on Learning Disabilities.

Mellard, D. F., Byrd, S. E., Johnson, E., Tollefson, J. M., & Boesche, L. (2004). Foundations and research on identifying model responsiveness-to-intervention sites. *Learning Disability Quarterly, 27,* 243–256.

National Association of State Directors of Special Education, Inc. (NASDSE). (2005). *Response to intervention: Policy considerations and implementation.* Alexandria, VA: Author.

National Center on Student Progress Monitoring (NCSPM). (2006). *What is progress monitoring?* Retrieved March 9, 2006, from http://www.student progress.org.

No Child Left Behind Act (NCLB). (2001). Public Law 107-110.

Pro-Ed Online. (2006). *Monitoring Basic Skills Progress.* Retrieved March 9, 2006, from http://www.proedinc.com/.

Stecker, P. M., Fuchs, L. S., & Fuchs, D. (2005). Using curriculum-based measurement to improve student achievement: Review of research. *Psychology in the Schools, 42*(8), 795–819.

5

Tier 1

General Education

R TI is a multitiered service delivery model. Although much discussion continues surrounding the issues of how many tiers constitute an adequate intervention, RTI is most frequently viewed as a three-tiered model, similar to those used for positive behavioral support (Vaughn, 2003).

The three-tiered model aligns the instructional needs of students with increasingly intense interventions in the same way the public health model is organized with primary, secondary, and tertiary intervention levels. Tier 1 is conceived of as the primary level of intervention implemented in the general education classroom. Tier 1 includes the research-based core curriculum, which all students receive. Tier 2 includes secondary interventions. Students who are predicted as having difficulty in Tier 1 or who have demonstrated that they are not achieving at the same level or rate as the class as a whole receive a more intense Tier 2 intervention to supplement the curriculum and instruction in the general education classroom, Tier 1. These secondary interventions are considered as short-term and target specific deficit skills or abilities. They are delivered in small groups of one to five students. Some students may not respond sufficiently in the secondary interventions of Tier 2 and need even more intense, individualized interventions. These most intense tertiary level interventions are included in Tier 3, which is synonymous with special education and the Individuals with Disabilities Education

Act (IDEA, 2004) protections for students with disabilities. See Figure 1.1 in Chapter 1, which depicts a three-tiered model as conceived in an RTI framework.

In multitiered models of service delivery, instruction is differentiated to meet learner needs at various levels. Several specific features distinguish the interventions at the various tiers, to include:

1. Size of the instructional group

2. Performance standards (mastery requirements)

3. Frequency of progress monitoring

4. Duration of the intervention

5. Frequency with which the intervention is delivered

6. Teacher or specialist training in the relevant content area

7. Focus of the content or skills

Some schools organize multiple levels of targeted, secondary-level, and tertiary-level interventions that are distinct from special education, which may result in more tiers in their RTI framework. A critical feature in any organization is that school staffs have a clearly stated framework for organizing their multiple tiers. That framework should include the dimensions on which the tiers can be distinguished.

Similar to other intervention models, RTI is meant to be applied on a schoolwide basis, whereby the majority of students receive high-quality, evidence-based instruction in Tier 1, the general classroom. Within Tier 1 instruction, schools can use special funding allocations related to the early intervening services provision in IDEA 2004. The early intervening services allow school districts to use up to 15% of their special education allocation for supporting students whose academic and behavioral difficulties limit their success in the general education classroom; these are students who are not identified as having a disability. Students who are at risk for reading or learning disabilities are identified through schoolwide screening for more intense support in Tier 2. Students who fail to respond to the interventions provided in Tier 2 may then be referred for an individualized, comprehensive evaluation, and, depending on the results, be considered for specialized instruction in special education.

In this chapter and in Chapters 6 and 7, all of which deal with the three tiers, we use these features as an organizing framework to describe the tier within an RTI model. Additionally, we discuss how screening and progress monitoring are integral components of the tiered model. Finally, we focus on the importance of data-based decision making and parental involvement in supporting successful RTI implementation. We provide case study examples at the conclusion of the chapter on Tier 3 (Chapter 7) to highlight how schools have implemented a tiered service delivery model.

Definitions and Features

What Is Tier 1?

As mentioned above (in this chapter and in Chapter 1), Tier 1 instruction occurs in the general education classroom. Here general education teachers deliver effective and engaging instruction in reading, writing, and math. It is beyond the scope of this text to prescribe effective instructional programs for all grades, across all content areas. Rather, we provide a framework consistent with the results of the research on professional learning communities (DuFour & Eaker, 1998) to assist schools in making these decisions. Several sources of information may be used to assist schools in determining what constitutes effective instructional practice at Tier 1 including (a) federal policy initiatives, (b) research related to the relevant academic area (e.g., reading), and (c) research and literature on effective schools and teaching. When these sources are used along with existing state and district curricular frameworks to inform, develop, and evaluate instructional delivery and subsequent student outcomes, the result is effective Tier 1 instruction. To illustrate how these sources may be used, we provide a brief example related to reading instruction.

Determining Effective Reading Instruction at Tier 1

School district staff have several resources to assist them in their organization of high-quality reading instruction in the general education classroom. Reading instruction should be aligned with recent policy initiatives, research on reading, and research on effective teaching of reading.

Policy Initiatives

As noted in Chapter 2, several recent federal policy initiatives, most notably the No Child Left Behind Act (NCLB, 2001) and its Reading First component, emphasize the use of scientifically based instruction to promote strong reading outcomes. These initiatives provide federal funding to schools that adopt a so-called scientifically based instructional program in reading, aligned with what have been identified as the major components of reading: phonemic awareness, decoding, fluency, vocabulary, and comprehension. Closely aligned with these initiatives is the requirement within IDEA that before a student can be considered as having a disability, there must be assurance that the student has been provided with appropriate learning experiences in reading. Two essential features of ensuring appropriate learning experiences are that the instructors delivering the instruction are highly qualified and that the core reading curriculum provides a sufficient coverage of the five reading components.

Research on Reading

The U.S. Department of Education selected 14 experts in reading research and instruction to form the National Reading Panel and gave them the task to review the existing research on effective approaches of teaching reading. The panel's review began with more than 100,000 studies but narrowed their focus to those studies that had clearly described instructional practices, used experimental designs, demonstrated a causal link between the instructional practices and learner outcomes, and had a large sample size. Since the publication of the National Reading Panel's report (National Institute of Child Health and Human Development, 2000), "Teaching children to read," the Bush administration's focus on what constitutes scientifically based instruction has come under increased criticism. In general, the criticisms highlight two notable deficiencies in the report that has informed federal policy: (a) the a priori decision to focus on the five components of reading (Pressley, Duke, & Boling, 2004), and (b) the narrow focus on experimental and quasiexperimental studies as the only research that can inform educational practice (Allington, 2003). A more comprehensive review of the existing research on reading highlights numerous related components that contribute to high reading achievement, such as strong language development (Scarborough, 2001), sustained use of reciprocal teaching strategies (Palinscar & Brown, 1984), and exposure to rich and engaging literature to promote strong cultural knowledge and critical thinking skills (Allington, 2003).

Research on Effective Teaching Practices Related to Reading

One major difference between research and practice in education is that, while researchers hope to isolate and control conditions and variables to understand the relationship one factor has on another, practitioners operate within complex environments in which they have very little control over factors that are important to researchers (e.g., random assignment of participants to treatments, reliability, applicability, validity, fidelity of interventions, skill level of the instructors, and narrowly focused interventions). One way that researchers hoping to understand more about effective teaching practices in general have sought to bridge this gap is through grounded theory research (Corbin & Strauss, 1990). Using this model, evidence of effective teaching is studied through observation, collection of supporting evidence, and careful analysis. In the reading literature, such research has identified that effective primary-grade instruction includes

1. Instruction in reading and writing skills

2. Reading of rich literature and developing strong written communication skills

3. Strong classroom management skills, such that most classroom time is spent on instruction (as opposed to discipline)

4. High motivation on the part of students, supported and encouraged by the teacher (Pressley et al., 2004)

5. Integration of curriculum, instruction, and assessment through the use of continual monitoring and adjustments in instructional practice (Southwest Educational Development Laboratory, 2000; Stecker, Fuchs, & Fuchs, 2005)

When these elements are used to inform and evaluate instructional practice at Tier 1, the RTI framework may be used to support both policy coherence (see Chapter 2) and higher student achievement.

Features of Tier 1 Instruction

In an RTI model, Tier 1 instruction is the base level of educational service delivery aimed at meeting the needs of most students in the school setting. Table 5.1 includes the tasks essential to implementing a rigorous Tier 1. The distinguishing features of this level within the RTI framework follow:

Size of the Instructional Group

Instruction is provided to the whole class. Results of existing research on class size at various grade levels should inform decision making. For example, studies in Tennessee, Wisconsin, and California have shown that class sizes in the range of 14 to 19 students in the early years result in higher achievement that is sustained in later years of schooling (Pressley et al., 2004).

Performance Standards (Mastery Requirements)

Most states have developed content standards across content areas and related grade-level equivalent (GLE) performance standards in reading, writing, and math. Performance in relation to these GLE benchmarks provides one way of determining student achievement. When screening measures predictive of later performance on the GLEs are adopted, performance on screens can help schools monitor and adjust instruction provided at Tier 1.

Frequency of Progress Monitoring

Recommendations on progress monitoring vary from as frequently as daily to as infrequently as four times a year. While research strongly supports the use of at least weekly monitoring (Stecker et al., 2005), emerging studies suggest that monitoring progress every three weeks provides sufficient indicators of student growth (Jenkins, Graff, & Miglioretti, 2006). Students identified on screening measures as being at risk should be monitored at a more frequent rate, with recommendations of weekly monitoring for a period of five to six weeks after the screen (Compton, Fuchs, Fuchs, & Bryant, 2006). Further results of progress monitoring should be evaluated at both the classroom and individual levels in Tier 1. Classroom performance provides an overall indication of the effectiveness of the instruction, whereas individual performance helps to identify students who should receive Tier 2 interventions.

Table 5.1 Essential Task List for Tier 1

Directions

In the second column, *Responsible Person(s)*, write the name(s) of the individual or team who will assume responsibility for the task identified in the first column. In the third column, *Timeline/Status*, write the deadline for the task or the status of the task.

Task	Responsible Person(s)	Timeline/Status
Identify research-based instructional programs and practices in reading, writing, and math.		
Select research-based curricula and interventions and resources to accompany core programs.		
Adopt a system to measure fidelity of implementation (see Chapter 8).		
Select and implement a schoolwide academic and behavior-screening program.		
Establish data collection systems and implement systematic monitoring of student progress to determine both performance and growth.		
Identify a team and a process for analyzing progress monitoring results.		
Develop decision rules (including cut score or zones) to determine which students are at risk and require further assessment or intervention, or both.		
Develop a program of continuous, rigorous, professional development experiences to support Tier 1 implementation.		
Develop and implement a process for collaborating with the problem-solving team and monitoring student movement between Tier 1 and Tier 2.		
Decide when to initiate parent involvement.		

Duration of the Intervention

Students remain in Tier 1 throughout the school year unless they are found eligible for special education and specially designed instruction that cannot be provided in the general classroom.

Frequency With Which the Intervention Is Delivered

Instruction occurs according to school schedules and curriculum guidelines.

Teacher or Specialist Training in the Relevant Content Area

Instruction is provided by general education teachers.

Focus of the Content or Skills

Instruction represents the range of content standards and related GLEs. In essence, Tier 1 represents a school's full instructional program (see Table 5.2).

Implementation

What Is the Role of Tier 1 Within an RTI Model?

Within a three-tiered model of RTI, Tier 1 represents the base level of instruction. Most students will achieve academic success when provided with high-quality Tier 1 instruction. As such, Tier 1 can help reduce the incidence of so-called instructional casualties by ensuring that students receive appropriate instruction accompanied by progress monitoring.

Tier 1 is particularly important for two reasons. First, it represents the first gate in a system designed to accommodate the diverse learning needs of all students. Thus, Tier 1 provides the foundation for instruction on which all supplementary interventions are formulated. Second, since Tier 1 focuses on all students, it is the most cost-effective means of addressing the population of learners. The subsequent tiers address the needs of fewer learners with additional resources. An important benefit of Tier 1 instruction is that when used in conjunction with universal screening measures, students who require more intense support are easily identified. Universal screening measures assess students' academic or behavioral skills or abilities that are predictive of learning and achievement. Additionally, results of

Table 5.2 Standards for Judging High-Quality Tier 1 Instruction

Directions

Read each of the standards that have been identified as mechanisms for judging high-quality Tier 1 instruction. The checklist is formatted so that you can indicate current and planned implementation.

- If the practice has been implemented, indicate that with a checkmark (✓).
- If the practice is being developed, rank by priority. Indicate 1 = of highest priority through 3 = of lowest priority. (Thus, practices ranked as "1" would be implemented before those ranked as "2" and those ranked as "2" would be implemented before those ranked as "3.")

	Status	
Standard	*In Place* (✓)	*Priority* (1–2–3)
Evidence-based practices consistent with the research and literature in the relevant content area are implemented.		
Teachers provide opportunities for differentiation, according to individual student needs.		
Multiple methods of representation, expression, and engagement are used to deliver instruction and assess learning.		
Progress monitoring of student performance informs teaching practice.		
Curriculum is aligned with relevant content standards and aligned within and across grade levels.		
General education teacher is highly qualified to deliver the instruction.		

SOURCE: Mellard & McKnight (2006).

screening and progress monitoring in Tier 1 provide school staff with evidence that can help inform decision making, such as determining requirements for professional development and required resources for delivering instruction.

Changing Structures and Roles

Alignment of the general education classroom to meet the definition and features of Tier 1 instruction will require significant changes to both school structures and individual staff roles. Tier 1 and the related requirements of universal screening and progress monitoring provide a useful framework for schools to align their school structures with effective school models, such as the professional learning community (DuFour & Eaker, 1998) and instructional program coherence (Newmann, Smith, Allensworth, & Bryk, 2001), in which curriculum, instruction, intervention, and assessment are aligned horizontally and vertically; teachers collect and analyze data to inform their practice; and schools work collaboratively to address the learning needs of both students (e.g., high-quality instruction) and teachers (e.g., professional development).

This approach represents a significant change in typical roles within the school structure. In Tier 1, general educators take a more active role in the screening and intervention processes of students determined to be at risk or not making adequate progress. The involvement of general education teachers in this process can help promote stronger collaboration; interventions can be designed that more directly support a student's ability to achieve in the general curriculum. Close collaboration promotes a seamless system of service provision that increases academic outcomes for all students (Learning Disabilities Roundtable, 2002). Table 5.3 divides school personnel into three main areas and describes some of the responsibilities they may be expected to undertake in Tier 1 instruction.

Challenges to Implementation

Because Tier 1 occurs in the general classroom, it is tempting to conclude that it is already being implemented. However, as described in this chapter, Tier 1 instruction is one level within a larger, integrated system of instruction, intervention, and assessment that provides IPC and promotes higher student achievement. Additionally,

Table 5.3   Changing Roles and Structures to Implement Tier 1

General Education

- Administer schoolwide screening measurements across content areas according to schedule.
- Administer assessments; chart and evaluate results.
- Identify students for further monitoring.
- Provide information to parents if using the results for reporting student progress.

Specialist and Support Staff

- Assist general education teachers in implementation efforts.
- Collect data on a screening tool and associated cut scores to inform the process.
- Collaborate with the general education teacher to determine which students require further assessment.

Administration

- Lead effort to create infrastructure for schoolwide screening.
- Provide necessary technology, materials, and resources.
- Provide initial and continuing professional development opportunities for new staff and refresher training for incumbent staff.
- Ensure fidelity of implementation through routine, periodic observation and discussions with staff.
- Research the availability of screening tool options with staff committee to select appropriate tools and methods.
- Incorporate this system so that it meets multiple requirements, including for example, determination of average yearly progress for NCLB (2001), and ongoing progress monitoring.
- Determine if classroom performance warrants intervention (i.e., entire class performance is considerably lower than other classes in the same grade level).
- Review aggregate data of classrooms with teachers and district personnel to inform decision making.

NOTE: *General Education* includes the general education teacher. *Specialist and Support Staff* includes special education, reading or learning specialists, related services personnel, and paraprofessionals. *Administration* includes building principals and assistants, as well as curriculum and/or assessment specialists at building or district levels.

Tier 1 promotes the adoption of research-based practices, which for some schools may require consideration of new instructional programs, evaluation of existing instruction, and reorganization of school resources. The challenges to implementing Tier 1 may best be categorized by the following:

1. Adopting and implementing research-based instructional practices across content areas

2. Aligning general education instruction both horizontally (across classrooms) and vertically (across grade levels), as well as with supplemental interventions (Tier 2) to promote the achievement of struggling learners

3. Relying on the general education teacher to conduct routine progress monitoring, review the results, and make required instructional adjustments

4. Implementing related universal screening measures as a routine part of Tier 1 to identify students who are at risk for the targeted academic area

5. Developing a system to monitor student movement through the tiers

6. Providing effective, continual, professional development to support and enhance teachers' technical, professional, and collaborative skills

Summary

RTI is built around a framework of high-quality instruction and formative assessments (screening and progress monitoring) that match learners' needs with research-based, appropriate instruction. Tier 1, which is the primary level of the tier structure, is designed for students in the general education classroom and through which the core curriculum in reading, math, and written language is delivered. A successful Tier 1 is an important foundation because it is the most cost-effective level of service and is the first gate for more intensive tiers of service.

Resources

Numerous resources exist to assist schools with Tier 1 implementation efforts. We have categorized the resources into four broad areas to provide logical starting points. The following resources may support your implementation of Tier 1 efforts:

1. Existing State and District Curriculum, Content, and Performance Standard Documents (Available from each state's education department Web site)

2. The Institute of Educational Sciences Regional Education Laboratory Program (http://ies.ed.gov/ncee/edlabs/)

The Regional Education Laboratory consists of a network of 10 laboratories that provide access to high-quality, scientifically valid, education research through applied research and development projects, studies, and other related technical assistance activities. Links to all 10 labs are available from the Institute of Educational Sciences site. In addition to focusing on specific content areas, the labs conduct research on effective schools, effective instructional practices, and effective school reform models.

3. National Councils and Associations in Content Areas

Professional organizations that develop principles and standards to guide content area instruction, assessment, and professional development include the following:

- **National Council of Teachers of Mathematics (http://www.nctm.org)**
- **National Council of Teachers of English (http://www.ncte.org)**
- **National Council for the Social Studies (http://www.ncss.org/)**
- **National Science Teachers Association (http://www.nsta.org)**
- **National Science Education Standards (http://www.nap.edu/catalog/4962.html)**

(Continued)

(Continued)

- **National Reading Panel**
  (http://www.nationalreadingpanel.org/)
- **International Reading Association**
  (http://www.reading.org)
- **National Center for Education Information**
  (http://www.ncei.com/)

4. Resources to Promote Effective Instruction for Reaching Diverse Populations

- **Access to General Curriculum and Universal Design for Learning: Problem-Solving Approach—CAST Teaching Every Student (2006) (http://www.cast.org/teachingeverystudent/tools/)**

  CAST is a nonprofit organization that works to expand learning opportunities for all individuals, especially those with disabilities, through research and development of innovative, technology-based educational resources and strategies.

- **Access Center (http://www.k8accesscenter.org/)**

  The Access Center is a national technical assistance center funded by the U.S. Department of Education's Office of Special Education Programs with a mission to improve educational outcomes for elementary and middle school students with disabilities.

- **National Clearinghouse for English Language Acquisition and Language Instruction (http://www.ncela.gwu.edu/)**

  This university-based clearinghouse collects, analyzes, synthesizes, and disseminates information about instructional programs for English language learners and related programs.

- **The Institute for Urban and Minority Education (http://iume.tc.columbia.edu/)**

  The Institute, which is based at Columbia University, conducts research and evaluation activities, provides information services, and assists stakeholders in program and professional development and evaluation for students in urban settings.

References

Allington, R. L. (2003). Accelerating in the wrong direction: Why thirty years of federal testing and accountability hasn't worked yet and what we might do instead. In R. L. Allington (Ed.), *Big Brother and the national reading curriculum: How ideology trumped evidence* (pp. 235–263). Portsmouth, NH: Heinemann.

Compton, D. L., Fuchs, D., Fuchs, L. S., & Bryant, J. D. (2006). Selecting at-risk readers in first grade for early intervention: A two-year longitudinal study of decision rules and procedures. *Journal of Educational Psychology, 98*, 394–409.

Corbin, J. M., & Strauss, A. (1990). Grounded theory research: Procedures, canons, and evaluative criteria, *Qualitative Sociology, 13*(1), 3–21.

DuFour, R., & Eaker, R. E. (1998). *Professional learning communities at work: Best practices for enhancing student achievement.* Bloomington, IN: National Education Service.

Fuchs, L. S., & Fuchs, D. (2006). Implementing responsiveness-to-intervention to identify learning disabilities. *Perspectives on Dyslexia, 32*(1), 39–43.

Individuals with Disabilities Education Act of 2004 (IDEA). (2004). Public Law 108-446.

Jenkins, J. R., Graff, J. J., & Miglioretti, D. L. (2006). *How often must we measure to estimate ORF growth?* Unpublished manuscript, University of Washington, Seattle.

Learning Disabilities Roundtable. (2002, July). *Specific learning disabilities: Finding common ground.* A report by the 10 organizations participating in the Learning Disabilities Roundtable, sponsored by the Division of Research, Office of Special Education Programs, Department of Education, Washington, DC. Retrieved April 11, 2006, from http://www.ncld.org/content/view/280.

Mellard, D. F., & McKnight, M. A. (2006). RTI implementation tool for reading: Best practices [Brochure]. Lawrence, KS: National Resource Center on Learning Disabilities.

National Institute of Child Health and Human Development (NICHD). (2000). *Report of the National Reading Panel. Teaching children to read: An evidence-based assessment of the scientific research literature on reading and its implications for reading instruction.* NIH Publication No. 00–4769. Washington, DC: U.S. Government Printing Office.

Newmann, F. M., Smith, B. A., Allensworth, E., & Bryk, A. S. (2001). Instructional program coherence: What it is and why it should guide school improvement policy. *Educational Evaluation and Policy Analysis, 23*(4), 297–321.

No Child Left Behind Act (NCLB). (2001). Public Law 107-110.

Palinscar, A. S., & Brown, A. L. (1984). Reciprocal teaching of comprehension-fostering and monitoring activities. *Cognition and Instruction, 1*, 117–175.

Pressley, M., Duke, N. K., & Boling, E. C. (2004). The educational science and scientifically based instruction we need: Lessons from reading research and policymaking. *Harvard Educational Review, 74*(1), 30–61.

Scarborough, H. S. (2001). Connecting early language and literacy to later reading (dis)abilities: Evidence, theory, and practice. In S. B. Neuman & D. K. Dickinson (Eds.), *Handbook of early literacy research* (pp. 97–110). New York: Guilford.

Southwest Educational Development Laboratory (SEDL). (2000). An introduction to the professional teaching and learning cycle. Retrieved November 21, 2006, from http://www.sedl.org/ws/ptlc.html.

Stecker, P. M., Fuchs, L. S., & Fuchs, D. (2005). Using curriculum-based measurement to improve student achievement: Review of research. *Psychology in the Schools, 42*(8), 795–819.

Vaughn, S. (2003, December). How many tiers are needed for response to intervention to achieve acceptable prevention outcomes? Paper presented at the NRCLD Responsiveness to Intervention Symposium, Kansas City, MO. Retrieved March 15, 2006, from http://www.nrcld.org/sympo sium2003/vaughn/index.html.

6

Tier 2

Intervention

As described in Chapter 5, RTI is conceptualized as a multitiered service-delivery model of prevention and intervention. In this conceptualization, secondary intervention (hereafter referred to as Tier 2) represents a critical juncture in the RTI process. Along with the scientifically based instruction at Tier 1, Tier 2 forms the school's line of defense for reducing the number of students who are low performing or inappropriately referred for special education programs. Providing timely and evidence-based instructional strategies to students at risk can be the difference between those at-risk students successfully returning to the general education classroom or being referred for special education evaluation (Compton, Fuchs, Fuchs, & Bryant, 2006). Therefore, a well-designed and well-implemented Tier 2 is essential to RTI, disability determination, and special education services.

In this chapter, we review the critical features of Tier 2, explain two approaches to implementation, and provide resources and activities for schools to use as a guide for implementation and monitoring.

Chapter at a Glance

Definitions and Features

What Is Tier 2?

Screening in Tier 1 can help to identify students who may be at risk for learning in a specific academic area. When a student's screening results indicate that he may be at risk for learning difficulties and keeping pace with his classmates, a school should continue to monitor his progress for a period of five to six weeks to determine if he responded well to Tier 1 instruction or if he is a "true positive" (Compton, Fuchs, Fuchs & Bryant, 2006). Students who remain at risk for failure (because they have not responded sufficiently to Tier 1 instruction) receive appropriate, evidence-based interventions designed to address specific areas of deficit. In addition, their progress within these interventions is monitored, and further decisions on their instructional program are made depending on the outcomes. This is Tier 2 intervention.

Students who receive Tier 2 interventions do so in addition to the instruction they receive in the general education classroom. Table 6.1 provides a list of standards for judging the quality of Tier 2 instruction. The listing helps school staff consider how well their organization of Tier 2 compares with features described in research. Tier 2 consists of general education instruction plus specialized intervention that includes the following features outlined by Vaughn (2003):

Size of Instructional Group

Tier 2 instruction is provided in small groups, about two to five students. Students are grouped according to area of need and skill levels as a way of allowing the school to maximize resources to provide quality interventions.

Performance Standards

Two indicators of performance are important: performance level and growth. Ultimately, the goal of a Tier 2 intervention is to help the student achieve grade-level performance benchmarks in the Tier 1 classroom, which requires close monitoring of student progress in Tier 1 as well as Tier 2 instruction. If a student meets performance levels in Tier 1, he may no longer require Tier 2 interventions. Because a Tier 2 intervention is targeted to support the student's particular area of skill, performance levels must be determined for the area of focus. Anticipated growth rates can be calculated based on existing evidence (where available) and goals determined based on time in the intervention. Students who make adequate growth may remain in Tier 2 until they also meet performance levels in Tier 1.

Frequency of Progress Monitoring

Although recommendations vary, monitoring of progress in both tiers typically takes place once to three times a week.

Duration of the Intervention

Tier 2 interventions should have a nine- to twelve-week duration and can be repeated as needed. This duration is needed in many interventions in order for them to influence student performance.

Frequency With Which the Intervention Is Delivered

Tier 2 interventions are typically provided three to four times a week, with each session lasting 30 to 60 minutes. School staff should note that intervention sessions of 60 minutes as opposed to 30 minutes have a large cumulative effect over a nine- to twelve-week duration and are a significant issue in judging the intensity of an intervention.

Instructor Qualifications

Instruction is conducted by trained and supervised personnel (and not by the general education teacher). For example, a qualified reading specialist or speech and language clinician would deliver a reading intervention.

Placement in and completion of Tier 2 interventions can result in one of three possible outcomes:

1. Successful progress is made in the area of deficit and the student exits Tier 2 to return to only Tier 1 instruction.

2. Although progress is being made, the student's overall performance in the academic area (e.g., reading recognition, fluency) is still below that of his peers. The student remains in Tier 2 for continuation of the intervention.

3. The rate and amount of progress indicated by progress monitoring or the level of support required for the student is judged as significantly different from general education peers or is so intense that referral for disability determination is warranted (Vaughn, 2003).

Implementation

What Is the Role of Tier 2 Within an RTI Model?

Tier 2 can serve different functions depending on the purpose of the RTI model. As part of a prevention and early intervention model, the purpose of Tier 2 is a stage in the process at which students at risk receive necessary interventions. In RTI models that serve as one component of the specific learning disability determination process, the purpose of Tier 2 is the stage at which nonresponders are identified and referred for further evaluation.

As part of a prevention and early intervention model, Tier 2 is considered an intervention intended to remediate the student's deficits and promote participation in Tier 1. As part of the specific learning disability determination process, Tier 2 interventions play an assessment role and address the question of how well a student responds to a specific research-based intervention. Therefore, if a student is performing at a lower level of achievement or is learning at a significantly slower rate than his peer group, RTI is used to determine whether inadequate instruction would account for this discrepancy.

Two approaches to structuring Tier 2 interventions have been described in the research literature: problem solving and standard intervention protocol (Fuchs, Mock, Morgan, & Young, 2003). Although the two approaches vary in their focus and implementation, the goal of both is to provide supplemental instruction to students for whom Tier 1 instruction is insufficient. Some schools incorporate a combination of the two approaches. Furthermore, in some implementations the two approaches occur sequentially with the standard intervention protocol occurring first.

Table 6.1   Standards for Judging High-Quality Tier 2 Instruction

Directions

Read each of the standards that have been identified as mechanisms for judging high-quality Tier 2 instruction. The checklist is formatted so that you can indicate current and planned implementation.

- If the practice has been implemented, indicate with a checkmark (✓).
- If the practice is being developed, rank by priority. Indicate 1 = of highest priority through 3 = of lowest priority. (Thus, practices ranked as "1" would be implemented before those ranked as "2" and those ranked as "2" would be implemented before those ranked as "3.")

	Status	
Standard	*In Place* *(✓)*	*Priority* *(1–2–3)*
Tier 2 interventions are research based.		
Tier 2 interventions differ from the curricular materials used in Tier 1 instruction.		
Tier 2 interventions begin as soon as possible after identification of those not responding adequately to Tier 1.		
In addition to Tier 1 instruction, students receiving Tier 2 interventions do so for at least 30 minutes each day (three to five times a week) for 9 to 12 weeks.		
Size of instructional group is no more than a one-to-five teacher-to-student ratio.		
Decisions about students repeating or continuing the Tier 2 intervention cycle are based on progress monitoring data.		
Appropriate instructional settings are designated by the school and include areas within the regular classroom, pod areas, separate classrooms, etc.		
Students may have more than one Tier 2 intervention cycle.		

SOURCE: Mellard & McKnight (2006).

Problem-Solving Approach (Individually Designed Instructional Package)

Many schools have a type of a problem-solving team, such as a student instructional team, multidisciplinary team, student study teams, or building assistance team. The purpose of these teams is to develop a plan for the instructional program in the general education classroom to support the targeted student, while simultaneously providing a positive effect on the instructional program for all students. In some instances, the targeted student's behavior might be an indication of problems in the instructional methods or curriculum directed at the classroom. Under an RTI service-delivery system, these teams would adopt a problem-solving approach that is based on student data and a continuing system of evaluation. These teams are most effective when learning and achievement problems are objectively defined, directly observed, and measured in the general education classroom (Kovaleski, 2003). This model emphasizes a behavioral description of the student's performance so that the behaviors can be quantified through repeated, well-defined measures such as those measures used in curriculum-based measurement.

The student's performance data are collected, analyzed, and used to develop hypotheses about the cause of the student's problem and the appropriate evidence-based strategies to remedy them. Furthermore, as the interventions are implemented, the student's progress is monitored at regular points in time. That is, the team continues to meet to discuss the outcome data and determine whether the intervention is having the desired effect, the specific intervention needs to be revised, or the student should be considered for further evaluation.

Some limitations of the problem-solving model include the lack of a strong evidence base that results in improved outcomes for students (Fuchs et al., 2003). In response to this limitation, best practice suggests that a problem-solving model is most effective when it incorporates the following attributes:

- A scientific approach to problem solving
- Interventions designed for an individual student based on scientifically validated principles of effective curriculum and instruction
- A system for continual monitoring/evaluation of intervention
- Collaborative relationships with general education and special education to develop, implement, and monitor the intervention

- Collection of information from a variety of sources, including teachers, parents, and others who best know the child
- Use of curriculum-based measurement to assist in problem identification and for continuing progress monitoring and evaluation of the effectiveness of the intervention
- Interventions embedded in the daily classroom routine so the classroom teacher takes responsibility for implementation (Kovaleski, 2003)

In this way, the problem-solving model mirrors the framework of the professional teaching and learning cycle (Southwest Educational Development Laboratory, 2005), in which teachers study, select, plan, implement, analyze, and adjust their instruction based on the needs of the students and the demands of the curriculum to support all learners. This framework becomes particularly important because these problem-solving approaches are not using validated protocols of interventions, so the efficacy of the intervention is unknown and must be carefully monitored.

Standard-Protocol Approach

Standardized protocols are interventions that researchers have validated as effective through experimental studies. Examples of a standardized protocol in reading, for example, include the use of explicit instruction to support students with decoding skills (see, for example, McMaster, Fuchs, Fuchs, & Compton, 2003; O'Connor, Fulmer, & Harty, 2003; Vaughn, Linan-Thompson, & Hickman, 2003), the use of strategy instruction to support students with comprehension challenges (see, for example, Kamps & Greenwood, 2003), or the use of fluency development to encourage more fluent reading of text (see, for example, Hasbrouk, 2006).

School staff is expected to implement research-based interventions to address students' difficulties. These interventions are not accommodations to existing curriculum that would modify the environment or task requirements such as extended time on tests, preferential seating, shorter assignments, or using a scribe or assistive technology. Rather, they are instructional programs aimed at remediating a student's specific skill deficit (e.g., phonological processing, math computations, and reading comprehension strategies). When selecting specific interventions, school staff must ensure that standard protocol interventions specify the conditions under which the intervention has proven successful, including the number of minutes a day, the number of days a week, and the number of weeks (typically 8 to 12) required for instruction with the intervention. Information about each research-based intervention also should describe the specific skills addressed, where the instruction should be provided, who should provide the instruction, and the materials used for instruction and assessing progress (Fuchs et al., 2003). These conditions are important because they provide the necessary information for ensuring that the intervention is provided with fidelity to address the student's deficit.

As noted above, many standardized protocols for reading have been developed. Work in math and writing is emerging. In the meantime, staff can select those interventions that best incorporate principles of high-quality instruction. Kavale (2005), Swanson (1999) and Swanson and Sachse-Lee (2000) provide guidance on effective instructional practices for Tier 2 level interventions. School staff should examine curricular options in light of these principles to inform their decisions about an effective curriculum or in choosing among alternatives. At the same time, these principles are about indicators of instruction, not curricular content or the scope and sequence of skills; curricular content must also be considered. Kavale (2005) found support for the following instructional techniques, which could be applied to a review of curricular materials to judge to what degree these techniques are incorporated:

- Self-monitoring
- Reinforcement
- Self-questioning
- Drill and practice
- Strategy instruction
- Feedback
- Direct instruction
- Repeated reading
- Error correction
- Formative evaluation
- Peer mediation
- Diagnostic-prescriptive instruction
- Peer tutoring

Swanson (1999) and Swanson and Sachse-Lee (2000) examined intervention studies that used single-subject or group research designs, and from their meta-analyses, a number of instructional principles consistently demonstrated their effectiveness. Included in their findings was that effective instruction incorporated elements of both direct instruction and strategic instruction. Interventions in the area of reading comprehension were particularly powerful when they used a strategic approach. Other principles for instruction that were most effective were those methods that incorporated one or more of the following:

- Sequencing (e.g., breaking down the task, providing step-by-step prompts)
- Drill-repetition-practice (e.g., daily testing, repeated practice, sequenced review)
- Segmentation (e.g., breaking down skills into parts and then synthesizing the parts into a whole)
- Directed questioning and responses (e.g., teacher asks process or content questions of learners)
- Control of task difficulty (e.g., the teacher provides necessary assistance or sequenced tasks from easy to difficult)
- Use of technology to provide additional practice and reinforcement of concepts (e.g., computers, presentation media, flowcharts)
- Small-group instruction (five or fewer learners)
- Strategy cues (e.g., reminders to use strategies, think aloud models)
- Supplement teacher and peer involvement (e.g., homework, others assist instruction)

These research-based principles provide school staff with information on which they can distinguish among the many options for curricula, most of which will claim that they are research based. The principles also provide guidance to problem-solving teams who are developing Tier 2 interventions. In addition, examples of standardized protocols for various content areas are listed in the resources section at the end of this chapter.

Changing Structures and Roles

Implementation of Tier 2 interventions requires significant changes to many staff roles and responsibilities and to school structures. Specifically, schools will need to

- Develop or adopt an aligned system of progress monitoring and screening measures to identify students who are at risk or not making adequate progress in the general education curriculum and, therefore, are eligible for Tier 2 interventions

- Identify scientifically based interventions across the academic domains that can be implemented as intended
- Adopt standardized protocols (i.e., reading intervention curriculum) that are scientifically based
- Adopt detailed procedures for consistent implementation of a standard treatment protocol or problem-solving framework for tiered intervention (Fuchs et al., 2003)
- Provide teacher and staff development to ensure sufficient staff to provide small-group instruction
- Adopt a system for continued progress monitoring and review of results along with set criteria for (a) exit, (b) continuation in Tier 2, or (c) consideration for movement to special education levels

The roles and responsibilities of various staff members will depend on the methods adopted by a school or district and the available staff. Table 6.2 provides a list of roles and responsibilities in a Tier 2 intervention model. Some school staffs might find these shifts in roles and responsibilities as significant and will need to provide extensive professional development (e.g., coaching, mentoring, and group support).

Challenges to Implementation

Historically, a significant issue facing schools has been the lack of resources with which to provide interventions and supports for students with low achievement. Because interventions require the work of specialist staff with low student-to-teacher ratios and a systematic process of data collection and evaluation, they will remain a resource-intensive component of the RTI framework. Thus, most of the challenges to implementation of Tier 2 stem from the demand for resources. More specifically, the challenges to implementing Tier 2 can best be categorized by the following:

1. Adopting and implementing research-based interventions across content and grade-level areas.

2. Aligning secondary interventions (Tier 2) to promote achievement in the general classroom for struggling learners. This may require a multifaceted framework that focuses on both remediation (Tier 2) and on accommodations to support learning in the general classroom (Tier 1).

Table 6.2   Changing Roles and Structures to Implement Tier 2

General Education

- Implement Tier 1 level instruction with fidelity.

- Evaluate and identify students as at risk and eligible for Tier 2.

- Depending on protocol adopted by school, provide Tier 2 interventions.

- Continue progress monitoring within Tier 1 of students in Tier 2 for comparison of growth with supplementary instruction and when supplementary instruction is discontinued.

- If another interventionist provides Tier 2 instruction, collaborate with that staff member on instructional methods used in Tier 1, monitoring of progress and incorporation of some of the intervention in the classroom to provide continued support for targeted students.

Specialist and Support Staff

- Provide Tier 2 instruction to small groups.

- Monitor progress of students within Tier 2 and analyze results as part of a consideration of (a) continuation of intervention, (b) exit, or (c) movement to increasingly intense levels of instruction.

- Collaborate with general education teacher to understand the Tier 1 instructional program and provide instructional or supplemental activities that can be embedded to provide additional support to targeted students.

- Promote either a standard treatment protocol or problem-solving model consistently.

Administration

- Provide resources for Tier 2, including appropriate reading intervention program, trained staff, systems for progress monitoring across tiers, and time for staff collaboration to make decisions about movement of students within the tiers.

- Lead the problem-solving model approach.

NOTE: *General Education* includes the general education teacher. *Specialist and Support Staff* includes special education, reading or learning specialists, related services personnel, and paraprofessionals. *Administration* includes building principals and assistants, as well as curriculum and/or assessment specialists at building or district levels.

3. Implementing a system of progress monitoring in both Tiers 1 and 2 and developing a coordinated system that allows for monitoring of individual student performance in both areas.

4. Coordinating schedules to allow staff review of individual student files and to allow interventions to take place.

5. Recruiting, funding, and training the required staff to implement Tier 2 interventions.

6. Providing effective, continual, professional development to support teachers' technical, professional, and collaborative skills.

Table 6.3 includes a listing of essential tasks for implementing Tier 2. A school district or school staff may use this listing to help their organization of Tier 2 procedures.

Summary

Tier 2 is the structure designed to provide instructional interventions for those students who are not learning and achieving at the same level or rate as their peers. In the research studies, Tier 2 is operationalized as a short-term (9 to 12 weeks) academic and behavioral intervention that focuses on remediating students' specific skill deficits so they can be successful within the general education classroom. These interventions are provided to small groups of students by someone other than the classroom teacher (e.g., by a reading teacher, speech and language pathologist, librarian, or Title 1 instructor). Important features of successful Tier 2 include explicit decision rules for selecting scientifically based interventions, judging students' progress, progress monitoring, and exit criteria. Tier 2 interventions might be individualized in a problem-solving model or selected from validated standardized intervention protocols. Even in the absence of validated protocols, interventions must incorporate principles of instruction and curriculum that have a scientific basis of efficacy (see, for example, Kavale, 2005; Swanson, 1999; Swanson & Sachse-Lee, 2000). Since Tier 2 procedures usually involve changes in decisions about students' instruction, continuing professional development opportunities are important—not only for developing instructors' skills, but also in helping all school staff adapt to the changing roles, responsibilities, and social interactions.

Table 6.3　　　Essential Task List for Tier 2

Directions

In the second column, *Responsible Person(s)*, write the name(s) of the individual or team who will assume responsibility for the task identified in the first column. In the third column, *Timeline/Status*, write the deadline for the task and/or its status.

Task	Responsible Person(s)	Timeline/ Status
Identify structure and make-up of problem-solving team.		
Select resources, curricula, and interventions for use with standard protocol approach in reading, writing, and math.		
Create and continue the development of resources on evidenced-based intervention strategies to support students.		
Schedule time for general and special education teachers to collaborate, observe, implement, and evaluate strategies.		
Develop decision rules (cut scores, exit criteria) for remaining in or moving out of Tier 2 (responsiveness versus unresponsiveness).		
Implement a system of data collection and progress monitoring for Tier 2 to determine level and growth rate.		
Provide professional development opportunities for problem solving and protocol approaches.		
Ensure time is scheduled and process is established for teams to meet and review student needs.		
Determine level of intensity of instruction for Tier 2 (how often, how long, size of instructional group).		
Identify measures and procedures to document fidelity of implementation of interventions.		

Resources

Numerous resources exist to assist schools with Tier 2 implementation efforts. In the following, resources have been categorized by content areas to provide appropriate starting points. The goal of this resource section is to provide the reader with specific examples of what constitutes a standardized protocol suitable for Tier 2 intervention. As work in various academic areas continues, readers are encouraged to evaluate new interventions according to the criteria provided in this chapter and the attributes of the examples provided. In addition, the U.S. Department of Education established the **What Works Clearinghouse (http://www.whatworks.ed.gov)** to assist in the objective, consistent review of scientific evidence regarding particular interventions. The Clearinghouse includes a list of topics (Beginning Reading, Early Childhood Education, Dropout Prevention, Elementary School Math, English Language Learners, Character Education, and Middle School Math Curricula) about which reviews are completed. It posts the results of those reviews so that consumer groups may make informed decisions. The following resources may support your implementation of Tier 2.

Reading

- **Benchmark Word Detectives
  (http://www.benchmarkschool.org/word_id_intro.htm)**

    This program provides students with the tools and strategies they need to become lifelong learners, thinkers, and problem solvers.

- **Center for Academic and Reading Skills
  (http://cars.uth.tmc.edu/projects/tpri)**

    This site contains several technical-assistance publications to assist schools develop, implement, and monitor reading programs.

- **Multicultural Reading and Thinking
  (http://www.ed.gov/pubs/EPTW/eptw10/eptw10k.html)**

    Multicultural Reading and Thinking is a development process designed to help teachers infuse higher-order thinking skills and multicultural concepts into the existing curriculum for all students, and to measure progress through writing.

- **Pearson Scott Foresman Early Reading Intervention (http://www.scottforesman.com/reading/eri/index.cfm**

  Based on Project Optimize, this program was designed for students at risk in kindergarten and first grade who need intensive intervention in phonological awareness, letter names, letter sounds, word reading, spelling, and simple-sentence reading.

- **Peer-Assisted Learning Strategies (http://kc.vanderbilt.edu/pals)**

  Peer-Assisted Learning Strategies (PALS) Reading and PALS Math enable classroom teachers to accommodate diverse learners and help a large proportion of these students achieve success. PALS Reading and PALS Math have been approved by the U.S. Department of Education's Program Effectiveness Panel for inclusion in the National Diffusion Network on effective educational practices.

- **Reading Partners Group at Washington Research Institute (http://www.wri-edu.org/partners/)**

  The Reading Partners Group is a research team dedicated to the development and dissemination of evidence-based reading instruction.

- **Reading Recovery Council of North America (http://www.readingrecovery.org/sections/reading/index.asp)**

  Reading Recovery is an intervention program designed to support first-grade students who have difficulty learning to read. Reading Recovery provides training, materials, and other professional development support to teachers.

- **Scholastic/Read 180 (http://teacher.scholastic.com/products/read180/)**

  This is an intensive reading intervention program that helps educators confront the problem of adolescent illiteracy on multiple fronts, using technology, print, and professional development.

(Continued)

(Continued)

- **Spell Read Phonological Auditory Training (http://www.spellread.com/)**

  This is a research-based, student-centered, results-driven reading and spelling skill development program that focuses on both the auditory and visual components of reading.

- **Strategic Instruction Model (http://www.kucrl.org/sim/)**

  Developed at the University of Kansas Center for Research on Learning, this is an integrated model that addresses many of the needs of diverse learners while helping teachers make decisions about what is of greatest importance, what can help students learn, and how to teach students well.

Writing

- **Access Center (2006) (http://www.k8accesscenter.org)**

  The Access Center is a national technical assistance center funded by the U.S. Department of Education's Office of Special Education Programs with a mission to improve educational outcomes for elementary and middle school students with disabilities.

- **CAST Teaching Every Student (http://www.cast.org/teachingeverystudent/tools/)**

  CAST is a nonprofit organization that works to expand learning opportunities for all individuals, especially those with disabilities, through research and development of innovative, technology-based educational resources and strategies.

- **National Center on Accelerating Student Learning (http://kc.vanderbilt.edu/casl)**

  This site provides information on interventions in reading, math, and writing for students with disabilities, with the goal of providing early intervention to provide a solid foundation for strong achievement in the intermediate grades and beyond.

Math

- **National Center on Accelerating Student Learning (http://kc.vanderbilt.edu/casl)**

  This site provides information on interventions in reading, math, and writing for students with disabilities, with the goal of providing early intervention to provide a solid foundation for strong achievement in the intermediate grades and beyond.

- **The Access Center (http://www.k8accesscenter.org/training_ resources/math.asp)**

  This center is a national technical assistance center funded by the U.S. Department of Education's Office of Special Education Programs. Information on math instruction and interventions are provided through publications, presentations, Webinars, and related links.

- **LD Online (http://www.ldonline.org/indepth/math)**

  LD Online provides information through its Web site related to LDs and ADHD. On this site, you will find resources related to math instruction and strategies that support students with math disabilities.

- **Voyager Learning, VMath (http://www.voyagerlearning.com/vmath)**

  VMath is an intervention program for students with math problems. VMath includes interventions along with appropriate progress monitoring tools.

- **Text-Based Math Resource (Stein, Silbert, Carnine, 2006)**

  This textbook emphasizes the direct instruction model, provides teachers with the information needed to design supplemental math instruction and to evaluate and modify commercially developed math programs, and gives teachers systematic procedures and teaching strategies to augment math instruction.

References

Compton, D. L., Fuchs, D., Fuchs, L. S., & Bryant, J. D. (2006). Selecting at-risk readers in first grade for early intervention: A two-year longitudinal study of decision rules and procedures. *Journal of Educational Psychology, 98,* 394–409.

Fuchs, D., Mock, D., Morgan, P. L., & Young, C. L. (2003). Responsiveness-to-intervention: Definitions, evidence, and implications for the learning disabilities construct. *Learning Disabilities Research and Practice, 18*(3), 157–171.

Hasbrouck, J. E. (2006). For students who are not yet fluent, silent reading is not the best use of classroom time. *American Educator.* Retrieved November 1, 2006, from http://www.aft.org/pubs-reports/american_educator/issues/summer06/fluency.htm.

Kamps, D. M., & Greenwood, C. R. (2003, December). *Formulating secondary level reading interventions.* Paper presented at the National Research Center on Learning Disabilities Responsiveness-to-Intervention Symposium, Kansas City, MO.

Kavale, K. (2005). Effective instruction for students with specific learning disabilities: The nature of special education. *Learning Disabilities, 13*(4), 127–138.

Kovaleski, J. F. (2003, December). *The three-tier model for identifying learning disabilities: Critical program features and system issues.* Paper presented at the National Research Center on Learning Disabilities (NRCLD) Responsiveness-to-Intervention Symposium, Kansas City, MO. Retrieved March 15, 2006, from http://www.nrcld.org/symposium2003/kovaleski/index.html.

McMaster, K., Fuchs, D., Fuchs, L. S., & Compton, D. L. (2003, December). *Responding to nonresponders: An experimental field trial of identification and intervention methods.* Paper presented at the National Research Center on Learning Disabilities Responsiveness-to-Intervention Symposium, Kansas City, MO.

Mellard, D. F. & McKnight, M. A. (2006). Screening tool for well-described responsiveness to intervention models and comparison models. Retrieved June 22, 2007, from http://www.nrcld.org/resource_kit/tools/RTI ScreeningTool2007.pdf.

O'Connor, R. E., Fulmer, D., & Harty, K. (2003, December). *Tiers of intervention in kindergarten through third grade.* Paper presented at the National Research Center on Learning Disabilities Responsiveness-to-Intervention Symposium, Kansas City, MO.

Reid, W. A. (1987). Institutions and practices: Professional education reports and the language of reform. *Educational Researcher, 16*(8), 10–15.

Southwest Educational Development Laboratory (SEDL). (2005). *Professional teaching and learning cycle.* Austin, TX: Author.

Stein, M., Silbert, J., & Carnine, D. (2006). *Designing effective mathematics instruction: A direct instruction approach,* 4th ed. Upper Saddle River, NJ: Prentice Hall.

Swanson, H. L. (1999). Instructional components that predict treatment outcomes for students with learning disabilities: Support for a combined strategy and direct instruction model. *Learning Disabilities Research and Practice, 14*(3), 129–140.

Swanson, H. L., & Sachse-Lee, C. (2000). A meta-analysis of single-subject design intervention research for students with LD. *Journal of Learning Disabilities, 33*(2), 114–136.

Vaughn, S. (2003, December). How many tiers are needed for response to intervention to achieve acceptable prevention outcomes? Paper presented at the NRCLD Responsiveness to Intervention Symposium, Kansas City, MO. Retrieved March 15, 2006, from http://www.nrcld.org/symposium2003/vaughn/index.html.

Vaughn, S., Linan-Thompson, S., & Hickman, P. (2003). Response to instruction as a means of identifying students with reading/learning disabilities. *Exceptional Children, 69*(4), 391–409.

7

Tier 3

Special Education

Within an RTI model as described in this book, Tier 3 is synonymous with special education: throughout the chapter, we use the terms *Tier 3* and *special education* interchangeably. Tier 3 represents an integral step within the RTI framework that aligns with other tiers and relies on a data-based decision-making model of instruction and intervention. For example, a student with reading disabilities may experience significant difficulties learning how to decode, even with Tier 2 interventions. Such difficulty is evidenced by the student's failure to demonstrate progress on the monitoring measures used in Tier 2. In other words, this student is a nonresponder and, therefore, requires more intensive intervention to make appropriate academic progress, including special education programming and placement. As such, special education (Tier 3) is intended to deliver the most intensive, scientifically based instructional programs to address individual student needs. Ideally, this tier is structured to provide flexible service, systematically permitting a student to move in and out as his needs change relative to the demands of the general education curriculum (Fuchs & Fuchs, 2006; O'Connor, Harty, & Fulmer, 2005).

In other RTI versions, Tier 3 is not synonymous with special education. Some RTI versions have other tiers in which group and individual interventions are delivered. One might think of those RTI models as "Tier 2 plus." Depending on a school's organization and resources, these additional tiers might be optimal. Our purpose in this chapter is to describe how special education services for students with disabilities might be distinguished—that is, to address how special education is different from other educational interventions.

Effective special education requires (a) identifying individual student needs, (b) setting goals that address educational needs specific to an individual with a disability, (c) implementing specially designed instruction to meet those goals, (d) monitoring and evaluating progress toward the goals, and (e) adjusting instruction when progress is unsatisfactory (Vaughn & Linan-Thompson, 2003). Instruction at this level is highly individualized, relentless, and iterative (Hallahan, 2006).

In this chapter, we provide a description of special education as an integrated component of the RTI framework, and present features of effective special education as described in the research. The chapter also includes a section entitled Tiered Service Delivery in Practice, which presents a case study of an integrated model of tiered service delivery implemented at the school level.

Definitions and Features

What Is Tier 3?

Tier 3, or special education services, provides scientifically based, individualized, iterative interventions to students with intensive needs who do not respond adequately to high-quality interventions in Tiers 1 and 2. Decisions about students' specific instructional needs are based in part on a student's lack of response to effective instruction. When a student is determined to have too low of a response at the earlier tiers, an individualized, comprehensive evaluation is conducted to determine whether the student has a disability. If a student is found to have a disability that affects his ability to progress in the general classroom, that student may be referred to Tier 3, or special education. Table 7.1 includes descriptive standards for judging high-quality Tier 3 interventions.

Special education can be defined as specially designed instruction to meet the unique needs of students with disabilities. To achieve academic success, students with disabilities require individualized, iterative (recursive), scientifically based instruction that is monitored on a continuing basis. Students with disabilities require a continuum of intervention options through general and special education across all grades and ages. Services may be provided through accommodations, modifications, intense instruction, and remediation. Whereas accommodations and modifications are generally provided to help the student with disabilities achieve expected outcomes in the general education setting, remediation and the development of compensatory strategies through intense instruction is the focus of special education interventions.

A key distinction between general and special education is that special education takes an individualized approach to instruction (Fuchs & Fuchs, 1995). Interventions in special education must be designed to meet the specific learning and behavioral needs of the student, implemented on a timely basis, provided by a highly qualified teacher or specialist, and monitored to determine progress and achievement of desired outcomes.

Specific forms of special education instruction that have been found to be most effective in teaching students with learning disabilities (LDs) combine direct instruction with strategy instruction (Swanson, 1999; Swanson & Sachse-Lee, 2000). A combined model includes explicit teaching of skills (direct instruction), along with metacognitive strategies that support a student's ability to learn independently (strategy instruction). Swanson (1999) identified several main features of a combined model that influence student achievement. These components of effective special education instruction are embedded within many existing curricula designed for use with students with LDs:

- Sequencing (e.g., breaking down the task, providing step-by-step prompts)
- Drill-repetition-practice (e.g., daily testing, repeated practice, sequenced review)

Table 7.1   Standards for Judging High-Quality Tier 3

Directions

Read each of the standards that have been identified as mechanisms for judging high-quality Tier 3 instruction. The checklist is formatted so that you can indicate current and planned implementation.

- If the practice has been implemented, indicate that with a checkmark (✓).
- If the practice is being developed, rank by priority. Indicate 1 = of highest priority through 3 = of lowest priority. (Thus, practices ranked as "1" would be implemented before those ranked as "2" and those ranked as "2" would be implemented before those ranked as "3.")

	Status	
Standard	*In Place* (✓)	*Priority* (1–2–3)
Tier 3 interventions are research based.		
In addition to Tier 1 instruction, students in Tier 3 meet for a minimum of two 30-minute sessions each day for at least 9 to 12 weeks.		
At least one special education intervention cycle occurs per semester.		
Size of instructional group is no more than a teacher-to-student ratio of one-to-three.		
Decisions about students repeating or continuing the special education intervention cycle are based on progress monitoring data and achievement of IEP objectives.		
Students may exit from special education intervention during the middle of the school year only if they demonstrate grade-level performance on specified benchmarks or progress measures.		
A student who has received previous special education instruction and has exited may re-enter Tier 3 as needed.		
Interventions in special education employ a combination of direct instruction and compensatory strategy instruction designed to remediate a student's targeted area(s) of deficit.		

SOURCE: Mellard & McKnight (2006).

- Segmentation (e.g., breaking down skills into parts and then synthesizing the parts into a whole)
- Directed questioning and responses (e.g., teacher asks process or content questions of learners)
- Control of task difficulty (e.g., the teacher provides necessary assistance or sequenced tasks from easy to difficult)
- Use of technology to provide additional practice and reinforcement of concepts (e.g., computers, presentation media, flowcharts)
- Small-group instruction (e.g., five or fewer learners)
- Strategy cues (e.g., reminders to use strategies, think-aloud models)
- Supplement teacher and peer involvement (e.g., homework, others assist instruction)

In addition to these instructional components, the critical features of special education in an RTI model follow:

1. *Size of Instructional Group.* Special education instruction is provided to individual students or small groups of up to five students.

2. *Performance Standards.* Special education programs, strategies, and procedures are designed and used to supplement, enhance, and support progress in the general curriculum by remediation of the relevant areas and development of compensatory strategies. Performance standards are determined by individualized education program goal setting and the results of the comprehensive evaluation. If a student is able to meet grade-level standards after a period of Tier 3 intervention, then she should be exited from Tier 3, although her progress should continue to be monitored in Tier 1.

3. *Frequency of Progress Monitoring.* Daily progress monitoring informs the teaching process at Tier 3.

4. *Duration of the Intervention.* Special education instruction will last considerably longer than the 10 to 12 weeks of supplemental instruction delivered in Tier 2, as determined by individual student performance and need.

5. *Frequency With Which the Intervention Is Delivered.* The frequency of special education instruction depends on student need.

6. *Instructor Qualifications.* Special education teachers deliver the instruction at this level.

Implementation

What Is the Role of Tier 3 Within an RTI Model?

The instruction and progress monitoring provided in Tiers 1 and 2 are an integral part of informing the intervention design and delivery within special education. Because a student entering Tier 3 will have received instruction at Tier 1 and most likely interventions at Tier 2, special educators and related service providers will have thorough knowledge of the instruction and interventions implemented to date and the student's response to those interventions. They can use that information to design interventions relevant to the student's learning needs. Additionally, general educators will be informed of the types of supports required in the general education classroom as students with disabilities receive accommodations, modifications, and remediation specifically designed for their individual needs. This information is important as students make a transition from Tier 3's intense service to the interventions and services provided in the general education classroom.

As currently practiced, placement in special education is often a terminal decision for a student: few students with disabilities exit the special education system. Tier 3 is meant to provide intensive support on an as-needed basis. Although a student may always have an LD, she may not always require services in a special education setting. The coordinated, tiered RTI model provides a continuum of service options, while the progress monitoring and resulting data-based decisions allow for movement among tiers. The flowchart in Figure 7.1 demonstrates how decisions for student movement in tiers might occur in an RTI framework. The process is meant to be recursive, so that assignment to a tier, even to Tier 3, is a decision that is revisited through routine review of student progress. When a student has reached the grade level equivalent performance standard, then she may be returned to Tier 1. Although many students will proceed from Tier 1 to Tier 2 prior to the comprehensive evaluation, not all students who are referred for special education will receive a Tier 2 intervention if their needs are severe enough to consider alternative placements.

Changing Structures and Roles

Changes are needed to implement special education as it is conceptualized in an RTI framework. If special education is to lead to beneficial outcomes for students with disabilities, teachers must be prepared to provide the most intensive, powerful interventions. For

Figure 7.1   Movement Through a Three-Tiered Model

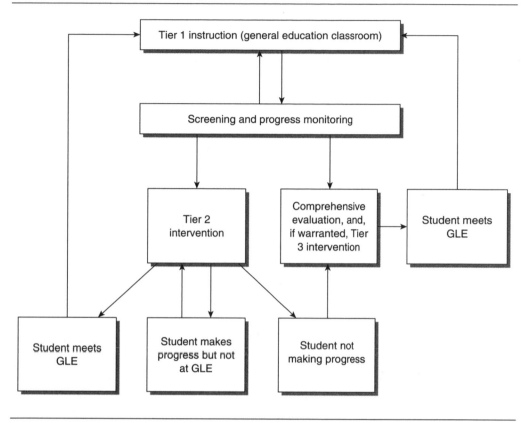

NOTE: GLE = Grade-Level Equivalent

most cases, teachers, both entry level and experienced, will need to receive further academic preparation in these methods. Since these interventions emphasize formative assessment, special education teachers will require administrative, technical, and practical supports to implement and sustain a system of continuous progress monitoring. Collaboration will continue to be an essential component of an integrated model of service delivery that supports the progress of students with disabilities in the general curriculum. Due to these realities, significant changes will be necessary in many staff roles and responsibilities as well as in overall school structures. Table 7.2 provides an overview of school staff's changing roles and responsibilities with RTI implementation. Three areas for scrutinizing current practice and possible improvements are as follows:

1. General and special education must be coordinated as part of a coherent system that is held accountable for the educational outcomes of students with disabilities.

2. School staff (general education, special education, administrator, and related service providers) must work collaboratively in planning and delivering interventions.

3. Principles, services, assessments, preservice training, and professional development must be aligned to result in a seamless system. (Learning Disabilities Roundtable, 2002)

The roles and responsibilities of various staff members will depend on the instructional methods adopted by a school or district and the available staff. Table 7.2 describes roles and responsibilities in a special education intervention model. The most significant shift in the framework for many staff members is the emphasis on the intensity of interventions for students in Tier 3. As suggested previously, these interventions target skill development in specific areas of reading, writing, math, and language. Our experience is that Tier 3 interventions require extensive training and coaching—and not a one-day workshop—in order to become proficient and comfortable with implementation.

By necessity, Tier 3 interventions will be delivered in small groups or individually to students and apart from the general education classroom. The hope is that, for these small numbers of students, the interventions will address the specific deficits that limit their success in the general education environment. The potential conflict is that current practices have an emphasis in supporting students in the general education environment. So, this restructuring of special education services for the neediest students will also require a shift in attitude for parents, teachers, support staff, and administrators. One of the most important supports for this shift will come from the progress monitoring data as interventions are delivered.

Even with general and special education staff working together to ensure a seamless system of high-quality services, the question remains: What is in the best interests of the student whose response to Tier 1, Tier 2, and Tier 3 instruction is limited? Does the student who is consistently a nonresponder receive special education instruction indefinitely? Should that student be returned to the more inclusive general education classroom to receive Tier 1 instruction with some supplemental special education instruction? If a student has a very limited response to the instructional offerings, are the student's rights to a free and appropriate education violated?

IDEA 2004 specifies that schools must provide a free appropriate public education, wherein the school provides special education and related services at no cost to the child or her parents in the least

Table 7.2   Changing Roles and Structures to Implement Tier 3

General Education

- Implement Tier 1 level instruction with fidelity
- Conduct progress monitoring of all students, including those in special education
- Provide appropriate accommodations or modifications for students with disabilities in the general education classroom
- Collaborate with special education staff on instructional methods used in Tier 1, monitoring of progress and incorporation of some of the intervention in the classroom to provide continued support for targeted students

Specialist and Support Staff

- Provide specially designed instruction to individuals or small groups
- Provide consultation regarding behavioral and instructional problems
- Provide expertise and guidance to parents, educators, and administrative faculty as members of the school-based support team
- Monitor progress of students within special education and analyze results as part of a consideration of (a) continuation of intervention, (b) exit, or (c) changes in intervention
- Collaborate with the general education teacher to develop appropriate accommodations/modifications that can be embedded within Tier 1 to provide additional support to targeted students

Administration

- Develop and oversee school-based instructional support team efforts
- Provide a supportive school environment that encourages collaboration
- Provide continuing, high-quality professional development to all instructional and support personnel
- Ensure adherence to timelines and cost controls
- Provide caseloads and schedules that facilitate individualized instruction, documentation of response to instruction, and collaboration among general and special educators, related services, and support personnel

---

NOTE: *General Education* includes the general education teacher. *Specialist and Support Staff* includes special education, reading or learning specialists, related services personnel, and paraprofessionals. *Administration* includes building principals and assistants, as well as curriculum and/or assessment specialists at building or district levels.

restrictive environment. At a minimum, schools should put in place procedures to document instruction and adequately monitor individual student progress in special education. For students who are unable to meet grade-level performance standards even with the most intense level of intervention, all of the available options must be carefully considered, including changes in targeted outcomes and alternative placements.

Challenges to Implementation

Many changes are occurring in special education, including increased emphases on outcomes as opposed to inputs in special education; an emphasis on access to the general curriculum; and expectations that all students, including those with disabilities, are included in standards-based reform. These changes challenge existing models of special education while facilitating implementation of an RTI framework.

The challenges related to implementing Tier 3 services may be organized in three main categories:

1. Meeting the high expectations of IDEA 2004 and NCLB 2001

2. Complying with the logistical and conceptual implications of adopting a data-based decision-making model

3. Ensuring adequate special education staff preparation and professional development

Both IDEA 2004 and NCLB 2001 establish high expectations for content and achievement standards that are the same for all students, including students with disabilities. Along with an increased focus on access to the general education curriculum, this legislation requires students with disabilities to be included in all general assessment programs, to be provided with specially designed instruction to meet the unique needs resulting from their disability, and finally, to be involved and make progress in the general education curriculum (IDEA, 2004). These requirements present new challenges for special education professionals, including how to develop an educational program that aligns with the general curriculum standards, yet remains flexible enough to address students' individual needs, goals, and progress, and that serves as a system that allows practitioners to enact individualized education. As school staffs consider their priorities in implementing or improving their existing special education procedures and practices, they may find Table 7.3 a helpful resource. This table includes a listing of essential tasks for Tier 3.

Table 7.3   Essential Task List for Tier 3

Directions

In the second column, *Responsible Person(s)*, write the name(s) of the individual or team who will assume responsibility for the task identified in the first column. In the third column, *Timeline/Status*, write the deadline for the task and/or the status of the task.

Task	Responsible Person(s)	Timeline/Status
Identify structure and make-up of problem-solving team.		
Select resources, curricula, and interventions for use with students with learning disabilities.		
Create and continue the development, individualization, and intensity of interventions to support specific student needs (how often, how long).		
Schedule time for collaboration among general and special education teachers.		
Develop ways to work as a team to deliver a comprehensive program of accommodations, modifications, or remediation to the targeted student.		
Develop decision rules (cut scores, exit criteria) for students remaining in or moving out of special education.		
Implement a system of data collection and progress monitoring to determine level and growth rate.		
Provide professional development opportunities for interventions with demonstrated effectiveness for students with disabilities.		
Identify measures and procedures to document fidelity of implementation of interventions.		
Develop a team of experts who use data to determine whether and when changes in individual student instruction are needed.		
Identify a team of experts who know which instruments and curriculum options are most likely to result in improved student outcomes.		

SOURCE: Mellard & McKnight, 2006.

IDEA 2004 places a strong emphasis on data-based decision making. Specific examples include regulations governing identification of students with LDs. As part of the eligibility determination process, data must be included that show the student received appropriate instruction in the general classroom (Tier 1) and that what appears to be a disability is not simply a result of inadequate instruction. As for the other tiers, the requirements for data-based decision making through frequent progress monitoring during Tier 3 pose significant challenges. Thus, research on the use of curriculum-based measurement in special education suggests that using progress monitoring results to inform instructional modifications has been difficult to implement (Stecker, Fuchs, & Fuchs, 2005). Even when the data are available, they are not used in instructional decisions about students.

Finally, in recent years, the role of the special education teacher has changed dramatically. Some special education teachers spend as few as two hours a week of instructional time with students due to other demands on their time such as program administration requirements associated with meetings (Hallahan, 2006). Others report feelings of professional ambiguity, unsure of whether their role is to tutor students in content areas or to provide specially designed instruction (Mellard, Deshler, & Barth, 2004). Many special education teachers have been providing the types of interventions that will be delivered in Tier 2 (secondary intervention) under an RTI framework. To successfully provide the type of intensive instruction required at Tier 3, they will need professional training and resource support within their schools. That support would include protecting their time, facilities, and materials so that they can provide the intense Tier 3 level interventions.

Tiered Service Delivery in Practice

The following case study describes tiered service delivery of reading instruction at an elementary school. The information was collected as part of a model site identification project conducted by the National Research Center on Learning Disabilities and has been included here with permission from both the Center and by Rosewood Elementary School, Vero Beach, Florida.

Rosewood Elementary School, Vero Beach, Florida

Overview and Demographics

Rosewood Elementary School has 549 students in kindergarten through fifth grade. Each grade level consists of four or five classes. Thirty percent (165 students) receive free or reduced-cost lunch, less than 3% (14 students) are English language learners, and 10% (53 students) receive special education services.

Rosewood Elementary's RTI model includes four tiers, with Tier 1 as the general education classroom, Tiers 2 and 3 as instructional support, and Tier 4 as special education.

Tier 1: General Classroom Instruction

The goal of Tier 1 instruction is to help all students achieve grade-level standards using a research-based core curriculum. The general education teacher uses the Harcourt School Publishers (2005) Trophies Reading Series for reading instruction during an uninterrupted two-hour block each day. Instruction is delivered to the whole class, as well as in small groups of seven to 10 students. The general education teacher uses Dynamic Indicators of Basic Early Literacy Skills (DIBELS; Good & Kaminski, 2002) to assess students in Grades K–1, and the Harcourt Holistic Assessments for students in Grades 1–5. If students do not meet grade-level benchmarks on these assessments, they move to Tier 2.

Tier 2: Intervention

The goal of Tier 2 is to provide small-group, evidence-based instruction to help students reach grade-level standards. The academic improvement plan team, which includes the general education teacher, the reading coach, and the elementary specialist, is involved with instruction, which takes place in the general education classroom. Instructional materials include the Harcourt Trophies Reading Series, as well as Earobics (Houghton-Mifflin Publishers, 2000–06), Road to the Code (Blachman, Ball, Black, & Tangel, 2000), Great Leaps (Campbell, 1995), and Quick Reads (Heibert, 2004). Tier 2 instruction is conducted for two hours in small groups of five to seven students in the general classroom, and generally lasts for nine weeks. Student progress in Tier 2 is monitored using Harcourt

(Continued)

(Continued)

Holistic assessments (Grades 1–5) and DIBELS (Good & Kaminski, 2002; Grades K–1).

If after the nine-week timeframe a student meets grade-level standards, she returns to Tier 1. If the student is making progress but is not reaching grade-level standards, she remains in Tier 2. If the student is not making progress in Tier 2 (as indicated by three consecutive data points below the goal line), she is placed in Tier 3.

Tier 3: Intervention

The goal of Tier 3 is to provide intensive, individualized or small-group, research-based interventions to support students' progress toward grade-level benchmarks. Tier 3 instruction can be delivered by the general education teacher, reading coach, student support specialist, elementary specialist, special education teacher, school psychologist, or speech-language pathologist. Instruction takes place in the general education classroom for two hours a day, with additional time, as needed, to address individual student needs. Tier 3 instruction is most often provided on a one-to-one basis or with small groups of five or fewer students.

Instructional materials are the same as those used in Tier 2, with individual interventions implemented to address any additional areas of concern. Progress is monitored on a weekly basis using DIBELS (Good & Kaminski, 2002), or AIMSweb Oral Reading Fluency or Maze (Edformation, 2006). When a student's rate of progress is not consistent with the desired goal after implementing two or more interventions, special education (Tier 4) is considered. Movement to Tier 4 is also considered when the student requires a high intensity of support that is not feasible for long-term implementation in the general classroom. Students considered for special education undergo a comprehensive evaluation to determine the nature of the disability and the associated services required. One can assume that students' limited response to high-quality instruction in the RTI tiers indicates that curricular and instructional factors can be eliminated and that a comprehensive review of the students' learning abilities is needed. The essential question becomes, What are the intra-individual and inter-individual differences that are limiting learning and achievement?

Tier 4: Special Education

Tier 4 instruction provides sustained, intensive support through a targeted curriculum for students with disabilities. The general and special education teachers share responsibility for instruction, which takes place in both the general and special education classrooms. Instructional materials for reading include the Harcourt Trophies Reading Series and Wilson Reading System (Wilson, 1988), with instruction delivered in groups of one to five students. Instructional blocks are two hours long, with additional time as needed to implement any supporting accommodations. Progress is monitored on a weekly basis using AIMSweb Oral Reading Fluency and Maze (Edformation, 2006), along with the measures described in previous tiers.

Professional Development

Rosewood Elementary uses a professional learning community model (see, for example, Astuto, Clark, Read, McGree, Fernandez, 1993; Hord, 1997) of professional development that includes a focus on various aspects of literacy across grade levels. District workshops on the five components of balanced reading (phonemic awareness, decoding, fluency, vocabulary, and comprehension) are scheduled every two weeks in conjunction with an early-release day for students. Additionally, the school uses instructor coaching to ensure faithful implementation of the interventions and to support teachers.

Challenges

Although Rosewood has developed a strong foundation for its RTI model, it still considers its RTI framework a work in progress. Many issues require continual investigation, which is well supported through the professional learning community model. Rosewood faces the specific challenge of having to develop a bank of interventions for Tiers 3 and 4 to support more intense student needs. Additionally, having to conduct universal screening and continuous progress monitoring requires innovative use of staff, parents, and volunteers.

Summary

A tiered model of intervention and a strong implementation of formative assessment are critical components of the RTI framework. When implemented with fidelity, a significant percentage of students will reach grade-level expectations through high-quality instruction in Tier 1. Furthermore, when Tier 2 interventions are designed and implemented in a way that aligns with the general curriculum, students who are at risk are afforded the instructional support they need to make adequate progress. However, with effective Tier 1 and 2 instruction, students with disabilities may require intensive support that can best be provided through special education services. Movement throughout the tiers is routinely monitored, based on individual progress and predetermined decision points, and remains flexible to accommodate individual student performance. A system of professional development that allows a school staff to learn together can enhance the implementation of the tiered model.

Resources

In addition to the resources provided in previous chapters, the following resources may support your implementation of special education within an RTI model.

- **National Association of Special Education Teachers (http://www.naset.org)**

   This organization provides resources and support to special education teachers. An extensive resource and publication list provides information on a variety of special education instructional methods and procedures. This site has limited access of materials for nonmembers and full access for paying members.

- **The Council for Exceptional Children (http://www.cec.sped.org)**

   The CEC is an international organization dedicated to improving educational outcomes for students with exceptionalities. This site has access to numerous resources and publications for nonmembers, with full access for paying members.

- **National Center for Learning Disabilities
  (http://www.ncld.org)**

   The National Center for Learning Disabilities is an activist organization that works to provide resources and information that support people with learning disabilities. Their Web site contains a variety of instructional and information resources for teachers, as well as links to current research in the field of learning disabilities.

References

Astuto, T. A., Clark, D. L., Read, A-M., McGree, K. & Fernandez, L. P. (1993). *Challenges to dominant assumptions controlling educational reform.* Andover, MA: Regional Laboratory for the Educational Improvement of the Northeast and Islands.

Blachman, B., Ball, E. W., Black, R., & Tangel, D. M. (2000). *Road to the code: Phonological awareness program for young children.* Baltimore: Paul H. Brookes.

Campbell, K. U. (1995). *Great leaps reading program.* Gainesville, FL: Diarmuid, Inc.

Edformation, Inc. (2006). AIMSweb. Eden Prairie, MN: Author.

Fuchs, D., & Fuchs, L. S. (1995). What's special about special education? *Phi Delta Kappan, 76*(7), 522–530.

Fuchs, L. S., & Fuchs, D. (2006). Implementing responsiveness-to-intervention to identify learning disabilities. *Perspectives on Dyslexia, 32*(1), 39–43.

Good, R. H., & Kaminski, R. A. (Eds.). (2002). *Dynamic indicators of basic early literacy skills* (6th ed.). Eugene, OR: Institute for the Development of Education Achievement. Retrieved March 26, 2006, from http://dibels .uoregon.edu/.

Hallahan, D. (2006, April). *Challenges facing the field of learning disabilities.* Presentation at the National Research Center on Learning Disabilities National State Education Agency Conference on Specific Learning Disabilities Determination, Kansas City, MO. Retrieved October 1, 2006, from http://www.nrcld.org/sea/presentations_worksheets/keynote/Out line.pdf.

Harcourt School Publishers. (2005). *Trophies Reading Series.* Orlando, FL: Author.

Heibert, E. H. (2004). *Quick reads: A research-based fluency program.* Parsippany, NJ: Modern Curriculum Press.

Hord, S. M. (1997). *Professional learning communities: Communities of continuous inquiry and improvement.* Austin, TX: Southwest Educational Development Laboratory.

Houghton-Mifflin Publishers. (2000–06). *Earobics*. Evanston, IL: Author.

Individuals with Disabilities Education Act of 2004 (IDEA). (2004). Public Law 108-446.

Learning Disabilities Roundtable. (2002, July). *Specific learning disabilities: Finding common ground*. A report by the 10 organizations participating in the Learning Disabilities Roundtable, sponsored by the Division of Research, Office of Special Education Programs, Department of Education, Washington, DC. Retrieved April 11, 2006, from http://www.ncld .org/content/view/280.

Mellard, D. F., Deshler, D. D., & Barth, A. (2004). SLD identification: It's not simply a matter of building a better mousetrap. *Learning Disability Quarterly*, *27*(4), 229–242.

Mellard, D. F., & McKnight, M. A. (2006). RTI implementation tool for reading: Best practices [Brochure]. Lawrence, KS: National Resource Center on Learning Disabilities.

No Child Left Behind Act (NCLB). (2001). Public Law 107-110.

O'Connor, R. E., Harty, K. R., & Fulmer, D. (2005). Tiers of intervention in kindergarten through third grade. *Journal of Learning Disabilities*, *38*(6), 532–538.

Stecker, P. M., Fuchs, L. S., & Fuchs, D. (2005). Using curriculum-based measurement to improve student achievement: Review of research. *Psychology in the Schools*, *42*(8), 795–819.

Swanson, H. L. (1999). Instructional components that predict treatment outcomes for students with learning disabilities: Support for a combined strategy and direct instruction model. *Learning Disability Research and Practice*, *14*(3), 129–140.

Swanson, H. L., & Sachse-Lee, C. (2000). A meta-analysis of single-subject design intervention research for students with LD. *Journal of Learning Disabilities*, *33*(2), 114–136.

Vaughn, S. (2003, December). How many tiers are needed for response to intervention to achieve acceptable prevention outcomes? Paper presented at the NRCLD Responsiveness to Intervention Symposium, Kansas City, MO. Retrieved March 15, 2006, from http://www.nrcld.org/symposium2003/vaughn/index.html.

Vaughn, S., & Linan-Thompson, S. (2003). What is special about special education for students with learning disabilities? *Journal of Special Education*, *37*(3), 140–147.

Wilson, B. (1988). *The Wilson reading system*. Oxford, MA: Wilson Language Training.

8

Fidelity of Implementation

M any failures of education reforms and practices can be attributed to poor implementation (Gresham, 1989). When schools
adopt new initiatives without fidelity to essential program design
features, the results are often discouraging (Kovaleski, Gickling, &
Marrow, 1999). Other chapters of this text provide information about
design features and how to implement RTI. This chapter focuses
on helping schools recognize how consistent and detailed measures
of fidelity of implementation support the efficacy of an RTI model.
Fidelity of implementation refers to how closely the prescribed procedures of a process are followed. Without fidelity to the process, it is
impossible to determine the cause of poor performance, which jeop-
ardizes the effectiveness of the RTI process.

The three-dimensional model of fidelity of implementation presented here can help schools ensure that RTI is implemented well.
A listing of resources to support these efforts is also provided.

Definitions and Features

What Is Fidelity of Implementation?

Fidelity of implementation refers to the delivery of instruction in the way in which it was designed to be delivered (Gresham, MacMillan, Beebe-Frankenberger, & Bocian, 2000). For example, a published reading curriculum may require teachers to teach decoding skills in a prescribed sequence and fashion. If teachers do not follow the sequence or the method, a student may not learn to decode accurately. However, it would be unclear whether the failure to learn was due to a problem with instruction (e.g., the teacher didn't follow the curriculum procedures) or a problem the student faces with learning. In an RTI model, fidelity is important at both the school level (e.g., implementation of the process) and the teacher level (e.g., implementation of instruction and progress monitoring).

Several studies on various interventions confirm the importance of fidelity of implementation to maximize program effectiveness (see, for example, Foorman & Moats, 2004; Foorman & Schatschneider, 2003; Gresham et al., 2000; Kovaleski et al., 1999; Telzrow, McNamara, & Hollinger, 2000; Vaughn, Hughes, Schumm, & Klingner, 1998). Specifically, the results suggest that positive student outcomes may be attributed to one of three related factors:

1. *Fidelity of Implementation of the Process (at the School Level).* In an RTI model, this refers to the consistency with which the various components are implemented across classrooms and grade levels.

2. *Degree to Which the Selected Interventions Are Empirically Supported.* If an intervention or instructional practice has a strong

evidence base, it is more likely to help improve student learning than is an intervention with an unknown outcome.

3. *Fidelity of Implementation of the Intervention at the Teacher Level.* If teachers do not implement the intervention in the way in which it was designed, students may not benefit, and a child assistance team may conclude that the problem lies with the student (as opposed to poor quality of instruction).

A Three-Dimensional Model of Fidelity of Implementation

When school staffs administer a standardized assessment, the assumption is that the test is administered according to the directions in the accompanying manual and that the examiner is appropriately qualified. Implementation of RTI must meet the same standard. As described in the research literature, direct and frequent assessment of an intervention for fidelity is considered to be best practice.

Descriptions of fidelity checks in the existing literature tend to focus on research perspectives rather than on practice. When researching the effectiveness of an intervention, it is critical to be able to report the fidelity with which it was implemented: (a) so that any resulting gains in student achievement can be accurately attributed to the intervention under scrutiny and (b) so that the intervention can be replicated. Similarly, when implementing an intervention, it is critical to know whether it is being implemented as designed, so that if the intervention is initially unsuccessful, schools can take appropriate measures to remedy the deficiency rather than abandoning the entire reform.

The ultimate aim of a fidelity system is to ensure that both the school process of RTI and the classroom instruction at various tiers are implemented and delivered as intended. This aim must be balanced with the school's existing resources. In recognition of this reality, we have conceptualized an approach to ensuring fidelity that is based on three dimensions. Figure 8.1 illustrates the model; each of the dimensions is described below.

- *Dimension 1: Method.* This dimension includes the tools and approaches a school uses to provide various kinds of feedback on how RTI is being implemented.
- *Dimension 2: Frequency.* How often checks are conducted will vary depending on the situation. A combination of approaches that includes annual, monthly, and, in some cases, weekly observations and review will provide the most thorough evaluation of how RTI is being implemented.

Figure 8.1   Three Dimensions of Ensuring Fidelity

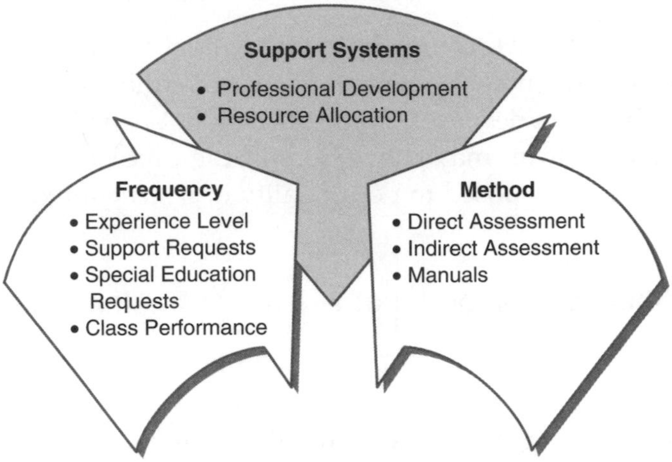

SOURCE: Johnson, Mellard, Fuchs, & McKnight (2006).

- *Dimension 3: Support Systems.* This dimension includes the feedback and professional development opportunities needed to implement a process with fidelity. Support systems should be selected and developed in response to school needs. For example, a school will need to develop professional development on their system of RTI for new staff, as well as a system of continued development in the instructional methods, interventions, and related assessments. An ongoing, flexible, and multifaceted support system will provide the best professional development response.

Implementation

Implementation of RTI places demands on a school's resources. Ensuring fidelity of implementation represents yet another demand. However, without fidelity checks, if RTI is not successful either in part or whole, it is difficult to take the appropriate steps to improve implementation, and the school may abandon the process altogether.

To keep fidelity manageable for schools, it is conceptualized here as a three-dimensional model that takes a proactive approach to implementing RTI the way in which it was intended. First, each of the three fidelity dimensions is explained. Next, we provide some indicators that schools can use to select the methods, the frequency with which they use the methods, and the support systems chosen to remedy areas of deficiency. Finally, we provide a detailed planning tool for schools to use as they implement the process to check fidelity of implementation.

Dimension 1: Method

Checking the implementation of a process for fidelity can be a complex and resource-intensive undertaking. In the research literature, checks for fidelity typically involve frequent observations and recording of behavior, teacher questionnaires, and self-reports or videotaping of lessons. The tools available to achieve fidelity may be divided into three main categories—direct assessment, indirect assessment, and manualized treatment (Gresham et al., 2000).

Direct Assessment

Using this approach, the components of an intervention are clearly specified in operational terms within a checklist, and a qualified staff member observes the intervention, counting the occurrence of each component to determine the percentage correctly implemented and identifying teachers who need retraining.

Indirect Assessment

Indirect assessment methods include self-reports, rating scales, interviews, and permanent products. Of these, permanent product assessment is thought to be the most reliable and accurate. Permanent products might include samples of student work or student performance on assessments. Each product would be related to a particular component of the intervention.

Manualized Treatments

Essentially, this represents a step-by-step guide or checklist to implementation. Although such guides are helpful in detailing the steps required for implementation, unless they are accompanied by completed checklists, accompanying student work, and assessment data, or one of the other methods included above, they are by themselves not sufficient for ensuring fidelity.

Direct assessments of an intervention are considered to be best practice because they provide immediate feedback on how instruction is being delivered. However, direct assessments are the most time consuming, so schools likely will have to prioritize the ways in which they plan to ensure fidelity of implementation of the various components of RTI. Many of the tools to begin a process of fidelity checks might already exist within a school or might be built into the RTI process. For example, classroom level reports of progress monitoring provide an indication of the number of students achieving at desired benchmarks. If a teacher has an unusually high number of students who do not meet benchmarks, this could be an indication that she requires support in delivering instruction, administering assessments, or other related classroom or instructional management process.

Dimension 2: Frequency

As mentioned above, the frequency with which fidelity checks are conducted will vary depending on several factors, including the following:

1. The experience level of the teacher

2. A teacher request for support in implementing a particular component of RTI

3. Overall class performance on progress monitoring, screening, and other assessments

4. The degree to which special education referrals do or do not decrease

As noted under Dimension 1 (Method), schedules for checking, reviewing, and analyzing data may already exist within a school or district and can be used in the process of checking for fidelity of RTI. For example, principals are required to evaluate new staff, state and district assessment results generally arrive at a given time in the school year, schoolwide screenings are routinely scheduled, child study teams meet on a regularly scheduled basis, and information on student performance and teacher instruction can be included as part of these meetings.

Table 8.1 lists different kinds of fidelity checks along a frequency continuum (from ongoing to annual) to demonstrate how this frequency dimension might operate within the larger context of fidelity of implementation. If used as a planning tool, it offers schools a comprehensive view of the amount, type, and regularity of feedback and data they are collecting on fidelity of implementation.

Dimension 3: Support Systems

As applied by schools, fidelity of implementation checks serve the purpose of identifying areas of strength on which schools can build and areas of deficiency that need to be remedied. For example, a

Table 8.1   Frequency and Fidelity Checking Methods Continuum

Task	Ongoing	Weekly	Monthly	3 Times a Year	Annually
Review state/district assessment results					X
Conduct screening				X	
Review progress monitoring		X			
Conduct teacher evaluations	X				
Solicit teacher comments/input	X				
Evaluate new staff				X	

newly hired teacher may not be familiar with the school's reading curriculum. This teacher might require professional development opportunities to become acquainted with the principles and procedures of the curriculum. Through previous fidelity checks, a teacher who is especially skilled with the particular curriculum may have been identified and can be paired with the new staff member to serve as a mentor or coach. At the class level, fidelity checks may reveal that a particular classroom may not have sufficient resources to implement and sustain a system of progress monitoring. This deficiency would require the subsequent attainment or redistribution of resources within the school. The kinds of support systems that are required to correct areas of deficiency likely will fall into one of two categories:

1. *Professional Development and Training.* This may include formal opportunities for workshops and inservice training, as well as for partnership with teacher mentors or coaches.

2. *Resource Allocation.* If teachers do not have the proper resources to implement the intervention, it is incumbent on the school leadership to obtain or redistribute resources.

Putting the Model Together

RTI represents a significant instructional shift for many schools that requires a coordination of processes at the school and teacher levels. Fidelity of implementation is critical for RTI or any education intervention to be successful. We recognize that schools have limited resources with which to implement the many initiatives and policy requirements they face. In this section, we have attempted to streamline the process of fidelity of implementation by noting indicators and applying the three-dimensional model (Table 8.2).

Table 8.2   Fidelity of Implementation Sample Application of the Three-Dimensional Model

Indicator	Method	Frequency	Support System
New staff has been hired.	Evaluations or observations.	Ideally three times a year, once early on.	Pair with mentor or coach; provide training in curriculum program.
Screening results show class averages are lower than school average, or a high percentage of kids are identified as at risk.	Review of data, direct observations, teacher logs, review any supporting evidence from parents, student work samples.	Same schedule as screening, with more frequent checks to resolve problems.	Have teacher work with mentor coach to problem solve, identify areas of strength and weakness; offer training opportunities.
Teacher evaluations highlight deficiency in instructional methods.	Follow-up observations, dialogues with other teachers, teacher logs/ self-reports.	As needed.	Identify problem to be able to either require professional development and/or allocation of resources.

Essential Task List for Implementation

Table 8.3 provides an essential task list for fidelity of implementation. While certainly not exhaustive, the list represents important steps in initial implementation. The first column describes the specific task required. The second column asks you to identify, by name, who has overall responsibility for overseeing this task. In some cases, more than one individual may be responsible. The final column allows you either to set target dates for completion or to indicate the status of progress related to the task.

Table 8.3   Essential Task List for Fidelity of Implementation

Directions

In the second column, *Responsible Person(s)*, write the name(s) of the individual or team who will assume responsibility for the task identified in the first column. In the third column, *Timeline/Status*, write the deadline for the task and/or its status.

Task	Responsible Person(s)	Timeline/Status
Develop a system of professional development and training as the school begins RTI implementation, and as the school hires new staff.		
Collect or create methods to ensure fidelity.		
Coordinate master schedules to conduct fidelity checks (e.g., teacher evaluations, walk-through checks, trainings).		
Develop a plan to systematically review results of information collected.		
Develop criteria to indicate when a teacher may require additional supports.		
Develop a plan to provide additional supports or professional development.		

Standards for Judging High-Quality Fidelity of Implementation

Methods of ensuring fidelity must be aligned with the requirements of the district, school, and curriculum. Therefore, we do not make any recommendations here on specific approaches. Regardless of the tools selected to implement and operate a system of fidelity, however, several criteria may be used to judge the quality of the system. Table 8.4 presents standards for judging high-quality fidelity of implementation that are based on the research in this area and that were used as part of a national effort to identify model RTI sites (Mellard, Byrd, Johnson, Tollefson, & Boesche, 2004). The checklist is formatted so that you can indicate current and planned implementation. If the practice has been implemented, indicate that with a checkmark. If the practice is being developed, rank its priority of focus; 1 = highest priority, 3 = lowest priority.

Fidelity of implementation is arguably the most important component of an RTI process because it serves as the means by which a school can evaluate and respond to professional development needs, resource acquisition and distribution, and infrastructure development.

Changing Structures and Roles

In an era of increasing demands for teacher accountability, a system of fidelity of implementation may be viewed as a negative development by school staff. However, ensuring fidelity of implementation can integrate the following three components of a school:

1. Instructional tools and strategies

2. Student achievement

3. Professional development

Such integration cannot occur if teachers are threatened by the system of observation and evaluation that accompanies this process. In many cases, accountability measures related to state assessments and NCLB (2001) have placed an emphasis on punitive measures for teachers. This need not be the case. Through the use of positive approaches to accountability, schools have the opportunity to implement a system of fidelity checks within a collaborative environment that promotes teacher improvement. As a part of that approach, accountability for implementation involves active participation and shared participation among teachers, administrators, students and

Table 8.4   Standards for Judging High-Quality Fidelity of Implementation

Directions

Read each of the standards that have been identified as mechanisms for judging high-quality fidelity of implementation. The checklist is formatted so that you can indicate current and planned implementation.

- If the practice has been implemented, indicate that with a checkmark (✓).
- If the practice is being developed, rank by priority. Indicate 1 = of highest priority through 3 = of lowest priority. (Thus, practices ranked as "1" would be implemented before those ranked as "2" and those ranked as "2" would be implemented before those ranked as "3.")

	Status	
Standard	*In Place* (✓)	*Priority* (1–2–3)
Specific, qualified staff member or members are designated to observe instructional methods.		
Staff members are trained in fidelity procedures and have authoritative status (i.e., can take action if necessary).		
To document fidelity of instruction, a teacher who is using a newly learned instructional method is observed immediately and then weekly or bi-weekly, as needed. A "master teacher" may be observed less frequently (three times a year or less).		
Classroom observation data are collected at least three times a year for Tier 1 and two times a year for Tier 2 to document implementation of strategies addressed in professional development activities.		
Observers complete a written checklist comprising the specific critical features of the instructional methods to document the degree of fidelity.		
Specific criteria (e.g., percentage of critical features observed) are used to judge methods as having or lacking fidelity.		
Feedback to instructional staff members includes one or more of the following: a scheduled conference, written information about problematic key features of the checklist, a plan for improvement, and a videotape of exemplary implementation with fidelity.		

SOURCE: Mellard & McKnight (2006).

parents (Neill, 2004). Honest and open communication with mentors or coaches, or both, can help a school tailor its professional development resources to support staff and ultimately improve student achievement. Evaluations and observations of teachers are approached in a positive manner that emphasizes problem solving rather than blaming. No important decisions about teachers, individual students, or the instructional program should be made solely on one type of evidence (Neill). Schools must be accountable for implementing procedures using information to guide decision making by teachers, students, parents, and administrators to improve the quality of schools and learning (Neill).

Teacher mentors also can play a larger role in the school environment to ensure fidelity. In order to make this process work, mentors or coaches must have authority to act. Mentors who have proven ability in the relevant area should be selected to serve as coaches to new staff. Mentors may require some training for their new role, especially if they now find themselves evaluating their peers.

Table 8.5 outlines some possible roles and structures for ensuring fidelity of implementation. Schools may choose to organize their process differently. For example, they may organize their process in ways that are consistent with their shared vision and implementation of RTI.

Challenges to Implementation

Although both common sense and research support the concept of fidelity of implementation to ensure an intervention's successful outcome, the practical challenges associated with achieving high levels of fidelity are also well documented. Gresham et al. (2000) noted several factors that may reduce the fidelity of implementation of an intervention, including complexity, materials and resources required, and perceived versus actual effectiveness.

Complexity

The more complex the intervention, the lower the fidelity of implementation. While many of the individual components of RTI are not complex, the coordination of numerous components into a seamless, integrated model presents challenges for schools. For example, the development, selection, implementation, and evaluation of Tier 2 interventions is a complex process that may require closer attention and scrutiny than implementation of screening measures.

Table 8.5   Changing Roles and Structures for Fidelity of Implementation

---

Teachers

- Collect the indirect assessments that can help corroborate manualized and direct observation results.
- Review existing checklists and manuals for implementation.
- Implement necessary changes to instructional practices (as result of faculty check).
- If requested, complete teacher reflections or teacher logs.
- If requested, videotape and review delivery of instruction.
- Review fidelity of implementation observation result with supervisor.

Mentor Teachers and School Coaches

- Monitor progress of teachers in delivering instruction in the content area.
- Provide professional development, coaching, and training.
- Evaluate results of observations and collected work samples to provide meaningful and specific feedback to teachers.
- Respond to teacher requests for assistance or information.

Administration

- Lead effort to create infrastructure for a cooperative fidelity of implementation process.
- Provide required resources to include access to the curriculum, opportunities to interact with mentors and coaches, and other material and equipment.
- Conduct teacher observations according to schedule and include the evaluation of evidence-based instructional practice.
- Monitor the special education referral rates and average class performance of teachers.
- Ensure fidelity of implementation through routine, periodic walk-throughs, observations, and discussions with staff.
- Coordinate for needed professional development.
- Determine if classroom performance warrants intervention (i.e., entire class performance is considerably lower than other classes in the same grade level).

NOTE: *Teachers* includes general and special education teachers. *Administration* includes building principals and assistants, as well as curriculum and/or assessment specialists at building or district levels.

Materials and Resources Required

If new or substantial resources are required, they must be readily accessible. Access includes both having the resources available (physical access), and providing the initial and ongoing support to teachers for their use (conceptual or cognitive access). Periodic reviews of material and resource requirements help improve and sustain implementation efforts.

Perceived and Actual Effectiveness

Even with a solid research base, if teachers believe an approach will not be effective, or if it is inconsistent with their teaching style, they will not implement it well. RTI represents a paradigm shift for many teachers. The focus on ongoing progress monitoring, the increased reliance on the general education teacher to provide support to students at risk, and the routine collection and analysis of data to support instructional decision making are all very different from what many teachers may have been trained to do. As a result, staffs will need to continue to discuss their perceptions of RTI and to be encouraged to openly communicate if specific components present significant challenges to their teaching approaches or philosophy. These discussions can help find workable solutions to implementation.

Schools are encumbered by numerous policy initiatives, increasingly diverse student needs, and limited resources. RTI has the potential to help a school make better use of its resources for increasing overall student achievement and for serving students with learning disabilities by the following:

- Allowing for early identification of students at risk through screening and progress monitoring, along with appropriate Tier 2 interventions.
- Aligning assessment procedures with instruction to develop a more comprehensive system of assessment to include both standardized measures and formative assessment of student progress.
- Providing multiple data points on which decisions are based to include screening results, regular progress monitoring data, and supporting student work.
- Ensuring access to appropriate instruction through the use of progress monitoring and evidenced-based instruction. Decision making is based on individual student needs as well as empirically supported practices.

However, these potentials cannot be realized if interventions are not properly implemented. Initially, ensuring fidelity will be a fairly resource-intensive process and will continue to require resources as schools receive new staff and students. We have attempted to consider the existing tools and procedures available to schools in developing a system of ensuring fidelity that supports but does not overwhelm schools as they implement RTI. As you read through the accompanying sample tools, you should consider additional resources that may have been overlooked in this chapter.

Summary

RTI is a schoolwide framework that integrates curriculum, instruction, intervention, and assessment. To be implemented well, it requires a strong collaborative relationship among school staff. Without assurances that instruction has been delivered as intended, that screening and progress monitoring tools have been administered with fidelity, and that related interventions have been provided consistent with the research base, the ability to support student learning will be compromised. Fidelity of implementation as described in this chapter is a way for schools to align a process of accountability with a supportive environment of professional development and growth.

Resources

The following resources may support your implementation of fidelity of implementation.

• **Washington State K–12 Reading Model Implementation Guide (Geiger, Banks, Hasbrouck, & Ebbers, 2005) (http://www.k12.wa.us/CurriculumInstruct/Reading/default.aspx)**

This document was developed by the Washington State Office of Public Instruction to inform the implementation of RTI to reading instruction. It provides details on assessment, intervention, and instruction, as well as checklists that may be used as part of a fidelity check of implementation.

(Continued)

(Continued)

- **Principal's Reading Walkthrough
  (http://www.fcrr.org/staffpresentations/SNettles/
  PrincipalWalkthroughContent.pdf)**

  This presentation and related documents (Nettles, 2006) were developed at the Florida Center for Reading Research, with individual checklists for kindergarten and first, second, and third grades. A thorough checklist of implementation at both classroom and school levels is included.

- **Intervention Validity Checklist (Vaughn, Linan-Thompson, Kouzekanani, Bryant, Dickson, & Blozis (2003)**

  The Intervention Validity Checklist was developed by researchers at the Texas Center for Reading and Language Arts in the College of Education at The University of Texas at Austin (Vaughn et al., 2003) to ensure (a) implementation consistency across teachers and (b) treatment fidelity.

- **Foorman and Moats (2004)**

  Foorman and Schatschneider (2003) and Foorman and Moats (2004) have developed observation protocols for measuring instructional effects on primary-grade literacy outcomes.

- **The Consortium on Reading Excellence
  (http://www.corelearn.com)**

  The Consortium on Reading Excellence has developed a number of reading-focused coaching and instructional implementation materials.

- **Fuchs and Fuchs (2006)**

  Fuchs and Fuchs (2006) identify dimensions and recommendations for RTI implementation in this publication.

References

Consortium on Reading Excellence (CORE). (2006). Retrieved March 9, 2006, from http://www.coreread.com/Downloads.htm.

Foorman, B. R., & Moats, L. C. (2004). Conditions for sustaining research-based practices in early reading instruction. *Remedial and Special Education, 25*(1), 51–60.

Foorman, B. R., & Schatschneider, C. (2003). Measuring teaching practices in reading/language arts instruction and their relation to student achievement. In S. Vaughn & K. Briggs (Eds.), *Reading in the classroom: Systems for observing teaching and learning.* Baltimore: Brookes Publishing Co.

Fuchs, L. S., & Fuchs, D. (2006). Implementing responsiveness-to-intervention to identify learning disabilities. *Perspectives on Dyslexia, 32*(1), 39–43.

Geiger, S., Banks, A., Hasbrouck, J., & Ebbers, S. (2005, January). *Washington state K–12 reading model: Implementation guide*, Office of the Superintendent of Public Instruction, Publication No. 05–0001, Olympia, WA. Retrieved on March 9, 2006, from http://www.k12.wa.us/curriculumInstruct/reading/default.aspx.

Gresham, F. M. (1989). Assessment of treatment integrity in school consultation and prereferral intervention. *School Psychology Review, 18*(1), 37–50.

Gresham, F. M., MacMillan, D. L., Beebe-Frankenberger, M. E., & Bocian, K. M. (2000). Treatment integrity in learning disabilities intervention research: Do we really know how treatments are implemented? *Learning Disabilities Research & Practice, 15*, 198–205.

Individuals with Disabilities Education Act (IDEA). (2004). Public Law 108-446.

Johnson, E. S., Mellard, D. F., Fuchs, D., & McKnight, M. (2006) Response to intervention: How to do it. National Research Center on Learning Disabilities, Lawrence, KS.

Kovaleski, J. F., Gickling, E. E., & Marrow, H. (1999). High versus low implementation of instructional support teams: A case for maintaining program fidelity. *Remedial and Special Education, 20*, 170–183.

Mellard, D. F., Byrd, S. E., Johnson, E., Tollefson, J. M., & Boesche, L. (2004). Foundations and research on identifying model responsiveness-to-intervention sites. *Learning Disability Quarterly, 27*, 243–256.

Mellard, D. F., & McKnight, M. A. (2006). RTI implementation tool for reading: Best practices [Brochure]. Lawrence, KS: National Resource Centeron Learning Disabilities.

Neill, M. (2004). Leaving no child behind: Overhauling NCLB. In Meier, D., & Wood, G. (Eds.), *Many Children Left Behind,* 101–120. Boston: Beacon Press.

Nettles, S. (2006). *Principal's reading walkthrough presentation and documents.* Florida Center for Reading Research. Retrieved March 9, 2006, from http://www.fcrr.org/staffpresentations/SNettles/PrincipalWalkthrough Content.pdf.

No Child Left Behind Act (NCLB). (2001). Public Law 107-110.

Rowan, B., Camburn, E., & Correnti, R. (2004). Using teacher logs to measure the enacted curriculum in large-scale surveys: A study of literacy teaching in 3rd grade classrooms. *Elementary School Journal, 105,* 75–102. Retrieved March 9, 2006, from http://www.sii.soe.umich.edu/documents/ EnactedCurr04.pdf.

Telzrow, C. F., McNamara, K., & Hollinger, C. L. (2000). Fidelity of problem-solving implementation and relationship to student performance. *School Psychology Review, 29,* 443–61.

Vaughn, S., Hughes, M. T., Schumm, J. S., & Klingner, J. (1998). A collaborative effort to enhance reading and writing instruction in inclusion classrooms. *Learning Disability Quarterly, 21*(1), 57–74

Vaughn, S., Linan-Thompson, S., Kouzekanani, K., Bryant, D. P., Dickson, S., & Blozis, S. A. (2003). Reading instruction grouping for students with reading difficulties. *Remedial and Special Education, 24*(5), 301–315.

9

Conclusion

R TI is proposed as a valuable model for schools because of its potential utility in the provision of appropriate learning experiences for all students as well as in the early identification of students as being at risk for academic failure. Students need and benefit from a close match of their current skills and abilities with the instructional and curricular choices provided in the classroom. When a mismatch occurs, student learning and outcomes are negatively affected. For some students, typical classroom instruction is appropriate and meets their needs. For some, however, such instruction does not lead to success. The hypothesis is that the sooner that struggling students are identified and taught appropriately, the higher the likelihood that they can be successful and maintain their class placement as underachievement is reduced or eliminated.

As described throughout this text, a strong RTI process includes the following critical features:

- High-quality, scientifically based classroom instruction
- Schoolwide screening of academics and behavior
- Progress monitoring of student performance
- Implementation of appropriate, research-based interventions at all tiers
- Fidelity checks on implementation

This text can serve as a useful guide for beginning the process of RTI implementation; even after reading this book, however, questions about the process are likely to remain. In this chapter, we present and answer some frequently asked questions about schoolwide implementations of RTI. Our answers draw from the experience of schools operating under an RTI framework that participated in a model site identification process conducted by the National Research Center on Learning Disabilities (NRCLD; Mellard, Byrd, Johnson, Tollefson, & Boesche, 2004). We conclude the text with some thoughts about overall challenges of RTI implementation.

Frequently Asked Questions About RTI

1. Why RTI and why now?

RTI has gained momentum as an instructional and assessment framework for a variety of reasons. As a framework, RTI is consistent with other tiered models of service delivery in public health and in some areas of education, such as positive behavior support. As a school reform model, RTI is consistent with other learning organization models, such as professional learning communities, and the professional teaching and learning cycle. As an assessment framework, nearly three decades of research on curriculum-based measurement and progress monitoring have informed both research and practice. Curriculum-based measurement and routine monitoring have consistently been shown to result in higher student achievement (Deno, 2003). RTI is also consistent with the focus on an integrated curriculum, instruction, and assessment model, also known as assessment for learning. Results of research on both instruction and interventions, especially in early reading, along with the recent focus on evidence-based practices also support the tiered model of instruction within an RTI model.

Within the field of special education, RTI presents a promising way to improve the identification of and service delivery for students with learning disabilities. Finally, as discussed in Chapter 2, the many recent policy initiatives at the federal level—including the No Child Left Behind Act (NCLB 2001), the Individuals with Disabilities Education Act (IDEA 2004), Reading First—and at the state level—align with the principles, components, and features of an RTI framework. RTI is consistent with the general focus on accountability, evidence-based practices, and data-based decision making.

2. As a school leader, where do I begin with RTI implementation?

One intent of this text is to serve as a guide to implementation at the school or district level or both. Most of the literature related to RTI focuses on early reading. The Reading First initiative, along with recent research reports on reading, to include the National Reading Panel's report (National Institute of Child Health and Human Development, 2000) provide a wealth of information on appropriate instruction, intervention, and assessment tools for use within an RTI model of reading instruction.

Additionally, since RTI is consistent with many policy initiatives, natural starting points and areas of alignment to facilitate implementation may already be in place. For example, the focus on accountability and progress monitoring in policy initiatives may provide a helpful starting point.

The research conducted by NRCLD on model site implementation of RTI has revealed that schools implementing RTI viewed the process as a multiyear commitment of initial implementation. (For more information on model sites, see NRCLD's Web site, http://www.nrcld.org.) Most sites began with a component that was already well developed. For example, some sites had screening and Tier 2 interventions in place. Other sites were using progress monitoring procedures. The sites then built on these strengths to organize the remaining components, such as tiered instruction and data-based decision making.

3. What are the professional development requirements for an RTI model?

As noted throughout this text, implementation of an RTI model requires major shifts in school structuring, as well as shifts in the roles and responsibilities assumed by school staff. In addition to training on specific components of RTI (e.g., selecting and implementing appropriate Tier 2 interventions), coordination of staff efforts and implementation, and training on infrastructure (to include instruction, curricular materials, assessment tools, and evaluation of data) will be needed on an ongoing basis.

Many sites that implement RTI design also implement embedded professional development as part of the RTI process. For example, at Northstar Elementary School in Knoxville, Iowa, routine professional development is provided by curriculum consultants for Open Court and Read Well. Other schools, such as Jefferson Elementary in Pella, Iowa, use instructional coaches or mentors, or both, to ensure fidelity of implementation and to provide an ongoing support system for teachers implementing RTI. Finally, other models of professional development, such as one in use at Rosewood Elementary in Vero

Beach, Florida, include an ongoing, integrated model conducted through the use of early-release days twice a month, and a coordinated effort at structuring professional development around the long-term issues related to RTI implementation. Rosewood Elementary also uses a professional learning community model to focus on writing and reading.

4. The current RTI literature focuses primarily on early reading. How does RTI work with other content areas and grade levels?

Although much of the literature on RTI is centered around early reading, a growing body of research is expanding the RTI framework to include math, the content areas, and higher grade levels (see, for example, Fuchs et al., 2005). The general principles of RTI will remain constant across grade levels and content areas. For example, Tier 1 instruction in math will include evidence-based instruction delivered in the general classroom. Related assessments for screening and progress monitoring will be selected and administered to identify students as being at risk for math difficulties (see, for example, Fuchs, Fuchs & Courey, 2005). Tier 2 interventions based on standardized treatment protocols in math (see, for example, Hot Math [Fuchs, Fuchs, Finelli, Courey, & Hamlett, 2004]) should promote skill development and knowledge in relevant areas. Students who fail to make progress despite receiving Tier 1 and Tier 2 interventions may be referred for a comprehensive evaluation for disability determination.

5. Is RTI a special education or a general education process?

RTI is a schoolwide process to integrate instruction, intervention, and assessment across the general and special education programs. The alignment of instruction, assessment, and interventions can help promote a stronger, more cohesive program of instruction that ultimately can result in higher student achievement.

6. How is RTI used within the process of specific learning disability determination?

RTI can help schools satisfy the requirements of IDEA (2004) regulations to provide evidence of appropriate instructional experiences, routine progress monitoring, and that a student has not responded to interventions. When used as a specific learning disability (SLD) determination process, it is imperative that RTI be implemented with rigor and that the assessments and related decision rules be based on current evidence and best practice. Because current applications of RTI do not address some constructs that are related to SLD determination, such as cognitive-processing deficits, our recommendation is that RTI serve as one component of an evaluation of SLD determination that also includes more comprehensive assessment of student functioning.

7. How does RTI differ from prereferral and building assistance teams?

Some of the literature on RTI suggests that it is synonymous with prereferral intervention. However, RTI is a more comprehensive framework for providing instruction, related interventions, and targeted special education for students at risk in the relevant content areas. RTI is a schoolwide process for bringing stronger alignment to the instruction and assessment practices of a school and is generally more proactive and comprehensive than the more reactive and individualized functions of prereferral and student study teams.

8. How does RTI let me know what to do to support student learning?

Because RTI is an integrated system of instruction and assessment, instructional decisions can be directly informed by the results of monitoring or screening. Critical caveats are that the measures are reliable and valid predictors of the skill or content and that instruction and interventions are implemented with fidelity. Although predetermined decision rules are important in an RTI framework, a knowledgeable staff and access to strong intervention resources are key in providing appropriate supports.

9. Can RTI be used for areas other than academic ones, such as behavior?

As mentioned above, RTI is closely related to positive behavior support models, and many schools are integrating the frameworks to attend to both academic and behavior support issues. Tualatin Elementary School in Tualatin, Oregon, for example, uses a continuum of schoolwide instructional and positive behavior support. Screening includes both academics and behavior to better inform the decision-making process and includes tools provided by Dynamic

Indicators of Basic Early Literacy Skills (2006), as well as data on attendance, behavior, and counseling referrals.

10. What role do and can parents play in the RTI process? When should parents be informed about their child's progress?

Parent involvement in a tiered service-delivery model is characterized by consistent, organized, and meaningful two-way communication between school staff and parents. In a school setting that implements an RTI model, parents should receive information about their child's progress, the instruction and interventions used, who is delivering the instruction, and what the parent's academic goals are for their child. Frequent communication with the school, receipt of regular information on student progress, and participation in decision making should provide parents the information they need if their child is referred for special education evaluation.

The following list provides standards for parent involvement in a tiered service-delivery model (Mellard & McKnight, 2006):

- Standards for parent involvement are aligned with IDEA (2004) regulations.
- Parental notification includes a description of the issue; clear, unambiguous documentation that shows the specific difficulties the child is experiencing; a written description of the specific intervention and who is delivering instruction; a clearly stated intervention goal; and a long-range timeline for the plan and its implementation.
- Parents and staff reach mutual agreement on the implementation plan and timeline.
- Parents frequently receive progress data.
- Parents are actively supported to participate at school and at home.
- School staff members strive to help parents feel welcome, important, and comfortable in the school setting.

At Jefferson Elementary School in Pella, Iowa, teachers use an intervention plan form to send home to parents. The form includes the name of the student, the area of concern, the grade-level targets and benchmarks, data collection procedures, and a plan for using the data for decision making. At the end of the form, there is a table for recording the instructional procedures, materials and arrangements used, the number of sessions a week and their length, individuals responsible, and follow-up notes. Additionally, Jefferson Elementary uses a Reading Plus Partnership Pledge for all students that outlines parents' responsibilities for supporting their child's learning (see http://www.nrcld.org/RTI_Practices/ for examples and more complete descriptions). This type of consistent and clear communication with parents plays a helpful role in supporting student learning.

Conclusion

Successful implementation of new practices requires attention in two primary areas: (1) understanding the specifics of the new practice and (2) identifying the values and context in which implementation occurs.

Specifics of RTI

In terms of specifics and details of implementation, the procedures and processes outlined in this text should serve as a helpful guide to begin the process. As more information related to other content areas becomes available, implementation following these procedures can be followed. Specific components of the RTI process that will require careful selection and monitoring include the following:

1. Thoughtful and Deliberate Selection of Assessment Instruments for Both Screening and Progress Monitoring

As noted in Chapters 3 and 4, screening and progress monitoring are critical components of the RTI framework. As such, it is imperative that the selected instruments have well-established reliability and validity for the relevant content area, and that staff charged with administering these instruments understand the uses, interpretation, and limitations of data derived from these systems.

2. Selection and Assignment of Interventions

Using a Tier 2 intervention to provide support for students identified as at risk can prevent academic failure. However, it is important that schools not fall into the trap of a "one-size-fits-all" approach to intervention. For example, standard treatment protocols are available for early reading. Many of these focus on interventions to target decoding, phonemic awareness, and fluency development. Reading, similar to math and writing, is a complex process that involves the integration of many processes, including language ability and background knowledge. Therefore, schools need to develop a range of Tier 2 interventions that meet a variety of needs and select and administer interventions for students based on specific, individual needs.

3. Fidelity of Implementation

The concept of fidelity is routinely mentioned in much of the literature on RTI. Unless a school implements the components of the RTI framework with fidelity, the process will not be helpful in preventing school failure, engaging in data-based decision making, or informing instructional practice.

4. Movement Throughout the Tiers

RTI can present significant challenges to scheduling and organization, especially when considering that students will be moving in and out of the tiered process. Developing an infrastructure to monitor student movement and progress, especially in larger schools, warrants careful consideration and deliberation.

5. Expansion to Other Content Areas and Grade Levels

Much of the work on RTI is currently focused on early reading. However, there is a growing body of literature on RTI's application to math and to later grades. Schools must continue their professional development as the knowledge base continues to expand.

Values and Context

Even when an education innovation is well defined, implementation, especially on a large scale, is not always successful. The challenges faced in bringing about institutional changes in education may be explained, in part, by recognizing that change will only be embraced and internalized if it is understood in relationship to the prevailing culture of the school setting and the perceived role of those who are expected to use the new process (Reid, 1987). While supportive policy and a well-designed process are necessary, they are not sufficient for bringing about improvement in school practices. A vital component is to also understand and address the perceived roles of key stakeholders (i.e., what role they see themselves playing. For example, if a fifth-grade teacher sees herself as responsible for teaching critical subject-matter content, she may be reluctant to take regular progress measures) and the culture of the school—whether it supports or presents barriers to innovations. Throughout this text, we have provided information on how roles, responsibilities, and organizing structures may change under an RTI framework.

As schools embark on the process of RTI implementation, a discussion of values and changes in roles and responsibilities may help facilitate the development of an RTI framework consistent with the goals and mission of the school.

RTI holds significant promise as a framework for organizing instruction, intervention, and assessment to promote higher student achievement. In addition to providing schools with a way to align their instructional programs, RTI also presents a way to provide early intervening services to students at risk for school failure and for schools to monitor and improve their instructional programs. Future research on RTI promises to expand the principles to areas beyond early reading, to include evaluations of various RTI approaches, and to address in greater detail the specific challenges of implementation. As research continues to inform the procedural aspects of RTI implementation, commensurate energy should be directed to understanding the contextual variables that play a significant role in shaping and influencing how RTI is ultimately implemented.

References

Deno, S. L. (2003). *Developments in curriculum-based measurement. Journal of Special Education, 37*(3), 184–192.

Dynamic Indicators of Basic Early Literacy Skills (DIBELS). (2006). Retrieved March 9, 2006, from http://dibels.uoregon.edu.

Fuchs, L. S., Compton, D. L., Fuchs, D., Paulsen, K., Bryant, J. D. & Hamlett, C. L. (2005). The prevention, identification, and cognitive determinants of math difficulty. *Journal of Educational Psychology, 97*(3), 493–513.

Fuchs, L. S., Fuchs, D., & Courey, S. J. (2005). Curriculum-based measurement of mathematics competence: From computation to concepts and applications to real-life problem solving. *Assessment for Effective Instruction, 30,* 33–46.

Fuchs, L. S., Fuchs, D., Finelli, R., Courey, S. F., & Hamlett, C. L. (2004). Expanding schema-based transfer instruction to help third graders solve real-life mathematical problems. *American Educational Research Journal, 41,* 419–445.

Individuals with Disabilities Education Act (IDEA). (2004). Public Law 108-446.

Mellard, D. F., & McKnight, M. A. (2006). RTI implementation tool for reading: Best practices [Brochure]. Lawrence, KS: National Research Center on Learning Disabilities.

Mellard, D. F., Byrd, S. E., Johnson, E., Tollefson, J. M., & Boesche, L. (2004). Foundations and research on identifying model responsiveness-to-intervention sites. *Learning Disability Quarterly, 27*, 243–256.

National Institute of Child Health and Human Development (NICHD). (2000). *Report of the National Reading Panel: Teaching children to read: An evidence-based assessment of the scientific research literature on reading and its implications for reading instruction.* NIH Publication No. 00–4769. Washington, DC: U.S. Government Printing Office. www.nichd.nih.gov/publications/pubskey.cfm?from=nrp.

No Child Left Behind Act (NCLB). (2001). Public Law 107-110.

Reid, W. A. (1987). Institutions and practices: Professional education reports and the language of reform. *Educational Researcher, 16*(8), 10–15.

Index